C. K F., F C. K.

Selection of Ballads

Translated Chiefly from German Authors

C. K F., F C. K.

Selection of Ballads
Translated Chiefly from German Authors

ISBN/EAN: 9783744781169

Printed in Europe, USA, Canada, Australia, Japan

Cover: Foto ©Thomas Meinert / pixelio.de

More available books at **www.hansebooks.com**

SELECTION

OF

BALLADS

TRANSLATED CHIEFLY FROM

GERMAN AUTHORS

PRIVATELY PRINTED

1873.

HE contents of this little Volume are composed of Translations from Foreign (principally German) Authors, made by the Compiler for his own amusement, in the course of two summer tours on the Continent. They have been printed for, and at the instance of, private friends, especially one to whose kind assistance and consummate knowledge of the German language he is indebted for any merit in the work; but he feels that he ought not to let them go forth without this acknowledgment, nor without apologies to the Authors of the original Poems for the indifference of the Translations, and for some slight departure, in a few instances, from the actual text. Generally the Translations are as literal as possible.

C. K. F.

Sept. 1873.

CONTENTS.

—◦◦⧉◦◦—

Columbus.

—∞:◦:∞——

" Fernando, why so serious ?" the great Columbus said,
" Bring'st thou bad news that thus thou com'st, with bent and hanging head ?"
" My noble chief thou judgest right, the crew's in mutiny,
" In headlong wrath they seek thy life, and come to bid thee die ;"
While thus he spoke, a crowd was heard, nearing the cabin door,
The rabble rout came rushing aft, with a mighty tempest's roar.
" Where now your hopes and promises, you perjured man ?" they cried
" Too long we've braved the stormy winds and ploughed the briny tide,
" Thus far like fools we've followed thee, and now we pine for food,
" Yet ere we die, we'll have revenge.   Traitor, we'll have thy blood !"
The ruffians said, but all unmoved, the hero gazed around,
And when he spoke, the roar was hushed, and silence reigned profound.
" Speak not of broken trust," he said, " the land is there, 'tis there,
" I see it with the eye of faith, if not in nether air,
" Yet hear me now, one compact more, 'tis but a little space,
" The night is settling on the deep, till morn I ask your grace."
His words, his godlike mien assuaged, the fury of the crew,
With downcast looks, and murmurs low, they yielded and withdrew,
Then sank Columbus on his knees and upward winged a prayer:
"Oh ! hear me Lord Almighty hear, the land I know is there,

" Oh, hear me, and their wrath abate, it irks me not to die,

" But all my cherished hopes to dash, my creed to falsify."

The night wore on, deep silence reigned, the stars in heaven were bright,

His gaze was ever westward turned, till dawned the morning light,

And when he rose, the glorious sun, and on a watery waste,

Without a sign of land, or shore, his slanting beams were cast,

The hero groaned, yet not for fear, but for a wasted life,

As uproar rose, and sounds approached, the sounds of coming strife.

The crew drew near, now traitor, now—prepare to meet thy fate,

They dragged him to the vessel's side, with scowls of scorn and hate :

The godlike hero knelt him down, he seemed as in a dream,

A cry was heard from the mizen top, " Land, land on the weather beam !"

And there beneath the western heaven, a narrow streak was seen,

Gilt with the sun's extending beams the sea and sky between,

The hero from his knees uprose, the crew sank down on their's,

There was an end of all his woes, an answer to his prayers.

LUISA BRACHMANN.

Calainos.

A MOORISH BALLAD.

—∞·ᴓ·∞—

The Moorish knight, Calainos, rode thro' the olive grove,
And as he rode, his eye surveyed, the royal towers above,
An aged Moor was pacing slow the battlemented walls,
" Now, gentle Moor," the knight exclaimed, " shew me the princely halls
" Where dwells the lady of my love, for whom 'twere joy to die,
" Sibyl Infanta fair, pride of all Paynimrie."
The lady from her casement looked, and smiling overheard
The knight's impassioned language,—she heard it every word.
And when the knight beheld the maid, his eye lit up with fire,
" Lady," he said, " I bring thee news, fresh tidings from thy sire,
" Almonzor brave, whom I have served seven years for love of thee."
Descending, then, the maid addrest the knight with courtesy,
" And who art thou, Sir knight," she said, " And by what noble name
" In courts and halls, to friend and foe, do thee thy deeds proclaim."
" Calainos, lady, is my name, lord of Arabia's land,
" The Turk, the Moor, the Saracen, acknowledge my command.
" To me the Grand Turk tribute pays, and holy Prester John,
" To me rich gifts and tribute come from mighty Babylon;

" Yet as a slave thy sire I serve, and cross the stormy sea,

" Encountering death in every form, and all for love of thee."

" Calainos, oh! Calainos," the royal maid exclaimed,

" You know not, oh! you know not, the boon that you have claimed:

" For he whose high ambition soars to have me for his bride,

" A thousand perils must incur—He must to Paris ride,

" And bring me back the heads of three,—three proud and valiant knights,—

" Peerless in fame for mighty deeds, first in a thousand fights,

" Orlando, nobly born and brave, the lordly Oliveiros,

" Ronaldo of Montalvan, too, three bold and mighty heroes."

Calainos, when he heard her words, bent low upon his knee,

" Sybilla sweet, Infanta fair, now give thy hand to me,

" That I may press it with my lips, in pledge that thou art mine,

" When low beneath my falchion's edge, the traitors lie supine."

The lady gave her solemn troth, and from the palace gate,

With joyful air the knight went forth, arrayed in princely state,

The crescent on his banners waved, his trumpets challenged loud,

And thus he entered Paris gates with mien and aspect proud.

Bound to the chase, the Imperial train had sallied forth that morn,

Ronaldo brave, and Oliveiros, Orlando nobly born,

And many a Paladin and Peer, and many a knight and squire.

Then rode there up a horseman bold, arrayed in Moor's attire,

" What dost thou here," the Monarch cried, " How dar'dst thou penetrate,

" Sir Moor, our royal realm of France, and enter Paris gate?"

" Sire," said the Moor, with dauntless mien, " I serve Calainos brave:

" He bade me, as his Herald here, thy royal favor crave,

" To challenge all thy lordly host, Prince, Paladin, and Peer,

" On foot or horse, with spear or blade, in arms to meet him here."

" Ne'er, in my youth," the Monarch cried, " such words were said to me,
" Nor stranger knight had unassailed, entered our fair citie,
" Now haste thee, tell thy master proud, Orlando shall him meet,
" And dead or living shall him bring, and lay him at my feet."
Then silently the Moor withdrew, and rose Orlando bold,
" My liege," he said, " Thou knowest well, nor needest to be told,
" Were twice a thousand Pagans here in arms I'd meet them all,
" But let this solitary knight to meaner weapons fall."
All silent were the peers of France, till youthful Baldwin rose,
" Orlando, as a peer of France, thy counsel I oppose ;
" Permit me, Sire, to meet the knight and give him quick despatch,
" A peer of France must ever be for any knight a match."
In vain the Monarch pleads, in vain,—his steed young Baldwin spurs,
To where the knight his onset waits, beneath a clump of firs.
" Now pause," the Moorish knight exclaims, " brave youth and be my page,
" And I will give thee lands and wage, a goodly heritage."
" Calainos, bate thine insolence," the noble youth replied,
" And meet me here in arms as now so proudly thou'st defied."
" Not so, fair Prince, to Paris speed, for if with me you fight,
" Pierced by my lance, you'll never see to-morrow's dawning light ! "
Swift at these words the youthful prince dashed on in mad career ;
The Moor, reluctant, met his charge, and foiled him with his spear,
Then leaping from his charger down, his scimitar he drew,
" Now tell me quickly, youth," he said, " Who art thou? tell me true."
" Baldwin, a peer of France am I, Orlando's sister's son."
" Then take thy life, and follow me, a captive's fortune shun,
" Orlando, then, and Oliveiros, Rinaldo, peers of France,
" Will meet me here in deadly fray, and fall beneath my lance."

Orlando from afar had viewed the ill-matched knights engage,
But when he saw his nephew's fate, he summoned quick his page,
And all in arms, with spear and blade, accoutred for the fray,
Across the intervening plain, eager he spurred his way.
With joy the Moor confronts his foe, " Who art thou, Cavalier ?
" Tell me thy name, and answer true, art thou of France a peer ? "
" Dog of a Moor," Orlando cried, " No terms I hold with thee,
" Release the noble youth from bonds, prepare to fight with me."
Then to the charge they fiercely rush, with deadly thrust and blow,
But soon the brave Orlando's sword, has laid Calainos' low.
Then by the beard he seizes him, " Tell me, thou Moorish spy,
" How did'st thou dare to enter France, and the twelve Peers defy ? "
" I love a noble Moorish maid," the prostrate knight replied,
" She bound her by her sacred troth, to be my lovely bride,
" When at her feet I laid the heads of Oliveiros true,
" Ronaldo proud, Montalvan, and brave Orlando, too."
" Calainos," said Orlando, " One—who laid such task on thee,
" Was little worthy of thy love, or knightly fealty;
" But for thine arrogance and pride, thou well deserv'st to die,
" Prepare thee, then, for instant death, nor ask my clemency."
And with the words he raised his sword, and with the trenchant blade,
Low on the sod his gory head, cleft from the shoulders, laid.
Then all the twelve applauded loud and uttered shouts of joy,
And hasted from his bonds to free the brave and princely boy.
And thus it was Calainos fell beneath the sword and lance
Of brave Orlando, noble knight, the mighty peer of France.

The Bard's Curse.

In ancient times a castle stood
　　　High on a table land,
Commanding all the country round,
　　　And the far distant strand,
Surrounded by a perfumed belt,
　　　A galaxy of flowers,
And watered by a thousand jets,
　　　Sparkling like rainbow showers.

A haughty monarch in the halls,
　　　Sat brooding on his throne,
In lands and conquests rich, indeed,
　　　Yet in his glory lone.
His thoughts were all of horrors dark,
　　　Fierce passions in his mood,
His words were all of vengeance dire,
　　　His judgments all of blood.

There came unto his castle once
    A noble looking pair,
One was a youth with golden locks,
    And one had snow white hair.
The old man bore a silver harp,
    And gallant steed did ride,
The blooming youth, in life's first spring,
    Tripped gaily by his side.

The old man spoke in loving terms,
    " Prepare, my son, I pray,
" Thy sweetest songs, thy mellowest tones,
    " For this eventful day ;
" Put forth thy skill, strain every nerve,
    " And summon all thine art,
" Haply to touch, by magic spell,
    " This monarch's stony heart."

And now within that noble hall,
    They stand, the minstrel pair,
The King is seated on his throne,
    Beside his Consort fair,
The Monarch, in his crimson robes,
    Is like the blood-red star,
The Queen, in snowy drapery,
    Like moonbeam from afar.

And now the old man strikes the chords
With such a magic power,
That rich and richer swell the tones,
Thro' hall, and roof, and tower.
Clear as a bell the stripling's voice
Warbles like evening bird,
While through it, as in angel choir,
The old man's notes are heard.

They sang of spring and love,
The joys of golden youth,
Of freedom—man's renown—
Of holiness and truth.
They sang of all that's bright and fair,
In this our mortal state,
And told of all the noble deeds
Man's heart could elevate.

The crowd of giddy courtiers, all
Forgot their empty jests;
The King's most mighty warriors
To Heaven they bowed their crests.
The Queen, in deep emotion plunged,
Of sorrow and of joy,
From out her bosom tore the rose,
And threw it to the boy !

Uprose the King in frenzy wild,
 His breast with passion rife,
" My people's minds ye have enthralled,
 With charms bewitched my wife !
He hurls his javelin at the youth,
 It penetrates his chest ;
Instead of golden song there flows
 His life-blood from his breast.

As by a mighty storm dispersed,
 The audience quick retired,
For, lo ! within his father's arms,
 The stripling has expired ;
And he, he wraps his mantle round,
 And sets him on his horse,
And from the castle turning sad
 He wends his weary course.

But ere he quits the postern gate,
 The minstrel takes his stand,
He grasps his harp, his matchless harp,
 The glory of the land,
He dashes it against the walls,
 It crashes on the ground,
While through the halls and castle yard
 His accents wild resound.

" Woe, woe, ye halls ! eternal woe !

    " Belong to you and yours,

" No songs shall ever more be heard,

    " Within your ancient towers ;

" But sighs, and sobs, and slavish steps,

    " And many a stifled groan,

" Till vengeance dark has worked your fall,

    " And crushed your every stone.

" Woe, woe, ye gardens, blooming now,

    " With all the flowers of May,

" Behold, with horror and remorse,

    " This cold, disfigured clay.

" Thus shall your blossoms withering fade,

    " And all your springs be dry,

" Soon shall your lawns and gay parterres

    " An arid desert lie.

" Woe, woe to thee, thou murderer,

    " Thou curse to minstrel art,

" The glories of thy house shall fade,

    " Thy earthly fame depart ;

" And all forgotten be thy name,

    " Lost in eternal night,

" Like artificial star, but now

    " That blazed with brilliant light."

He spake, the brave old man,
  Heaven heard his righteous doom,
In ruin lie those castle towers,
  Its halls are steeped in gloom.
One only marble column tells,
  Of splendour past away,
And this has felt the storm, and fast
  Lies crumbling to decay.

Instead of perfumed gardens now,
  All is a desert land ;
No tree doth lend its kindly shade,
  No fountains pierce the sand.
For, lo ! the minstrel's curse is heard,
  And lost to mortal fame,
No bard shall sing, no lay shall breathe
  That monarch's hated name.

        UHLAND.

Leonora.

From restless dreams fair Leonore
Rose to her daily cares once more,
"Art thou faithless?   Art thou dead?
"William, my true love!" she said;
For in King Frederick's bloody war,
To Prague's stern battle he had gone,
And to his fair Leonore,
Word of love had written none.

The Empress and the King at length,
Their wrath exhausted, and their strength,
With softened hearts at last made peace,
And gave their weary troops release.
And the armies, glad and joyous,
To their homes returned victorious,
Colours flying, trumpets sounding,
Every heart with rapture bounding.

In every house, in every place,
Gladness reigned on every face,
Old and young, with songs of joy,
Hailed the Victors, man and boy.
Thanks to Heaven went up for life,
From many a parent, child, and wife,
But for Leonora lone,
Was there kiss or greeting none.

Oft she asked, and asked in vain,
Many a warrior 'mong the train ;
None of all that mighty host,
Could give tidings of her lost.
And now that all the crowd are gone,
And Leonora left alone,
She threw her down and tore her hair,
With gesstures wild, in mad despair.

Her mother hasted to her side,
She caught her in her arms and cried,
" My child ! my child ! what ails thee, say,
" Have pity on her, Lord, I pray."
" Oh ! mother, mother, all is lost,
" To dark despair my soul is driven ;
" My mind is racked and tempest tost,
" For me no mercy is in Heaven."

" Now, God forgive her! Oh ! my child,

" For patience pray, and grace, and light,

" For God is full of mercy mild,

" And all he does is good and right."

" Oh ! mother, say not so, for what

" Have all my vows and prayers availed ?

" Heaven has denounced my wretched lot,

" And all my hopes on earth have failed."

" Heaven help her ! Oh ! bethink thee child,

" The Church's sacraments will calm,

" Will soothe and tame these passions wild,

" And give thy wounded spirit balm."

" Oh ! mother, all too deep my woes,

" For any leech to heal or close,

" The Church can me no comfort give,

" It cannot bid the dead to live."

" My, child, if thy betrothed be slain,

" 'Tis vain to wish him back again ;

" But if to thee he faithless be,

" God will avenge his perjury.

" Abjure the false one— be content ;

" God will award him punishment."

" Oh ! mother, mother, lost is lost,

" And gone is gone for ever ;

" A shadow dark my life has cros't,

" The sun shall gild it never

" Would that I never had been born,

" Wretched, disconsolate, forlorn,

" Death is my fate, and misery,

" For Heaven has mercy none for me."

" Help her, Oh, God ! Oh, help my child ;

" Pardon her sin—her passions wild.

" Her thoughtless words remember not,

" Have pity on her hapless lot.

" And thou, my child, forget thy sorrow,

" The blackest midnight has a morrow.

" And He, in Heaven, who pities thee,

" The Bridegroom of thy Soul will be "

" Oh ! mother, mother, what is Heaven ?

" Oh ! mother, what is Hell ?

" Without my William, what were Heaven ?

" Or with him, what were Hell ?

" In cloud, and mist, and darkness let

" The sun of my existence set.

" Without my William, earth were naught,

" Without him, Heaven were dearly bought ! "

'Twas thus the hapless maiden raged,
Thus war with Heaven's decrees she waged ;
She wrung her hands and struck her breast,
Till sank the glorious sun to rest,
And stars began to shimmer through
Heaven's vaulted arch of azure blue.

'Tis night, the tramp of steed is nigh—
The clash of arms—a knight rides by ;
The clang of drawbridge, clank of spur,
And measured tread the night air stir,
Gently, softly, clink, clink, clink,
Thro' the oaken doorway chink ;
A knight dismounts and treads the stair,
And, hark, a voice is calling there.

" Hollah ! hollah ! my love, my bride,
" Open the portal, open wide ;
" Art thou waking, art thou sleeping ?
" Smiling sweet, or sadly weeping ? "
" Ah ! William, is it thou ? " she said,
" Whence com'st thou, say, and why so late ?
" Thro' weary days and nights I've prayed,
" And wrestled with the laws of fate."

" My love, my love, I've ridden far,
" We saddled with the evening star;
" I've come to bear thee to my home,
" 'Tis late, 'tis late, my loved one come."
" Oh! William, enter quick my love,
" The wind is whistling through the grove,
" Come to my arms, beloved, come,
" My heart, my bosom, are thy home."

" The wind, my child, oh, let it blow,
" My black steed paws the ground below;
" I may not linger here—The night
" Is waning fast, the moon shines bright;
" Come doff thy train and mount behind
" My charger, swifter than the wind,
" For we a hundred miles must ride,
" Ere I can claim thee for my bride."

" What! must we ride a hundred miles,
" Ere fate upon our bridal smiles?
" Nay, but the bell now sounds the hour,
" Eleven upon the belfry tower."
" My love, look here! my love, look here!
" The moon shines bright, the moon shines clear;
" We, and the dead, we travel fast,
" We'll reach the goal, ere night be past."

" But tell me where shall be our home,
" Where to thy arms thy bride may come ?"
" My love, 'tis far away," he said,
" Our nuptial couch is duly spread.
" Six feet by two" " is room for me ?"
" Nay, room enough for me and thee ;
" So mount my steed, the bridal waits,
" The wedding guests are at the gates."

The maiden loosed her train and sprang
To the steed's back ; his trappings rang:
Her lily arms she closely wound
Her true knight's belted waist around ;
Hoorah ! hoorah ! with snort and stamp,
The steed's hoofs echo, tramp, tramp, tramp,
And scatter sparks, and pebbles throw,
As at mad gallop wild they go.

To right and left, before their sight,
Pastures and forests wing their flight ;
The bridges clatter, " Dost thou fear ?
" My love, my love, the moon shines clear.
" Hoorah ! the dead ride fast," he said ;
" My love, and dost thou fear the dead ?"
" Oh, no ! but speak not of the dead."

But hark ! there sounds a dismal moan,
Seems it a dirge or dying groan ?
The ravens flap their wings,—a bell,
Tolls a departed mortal's knell.
And near approaches and more near,
A coffin dark, with pall and bier;
Mid mutterings harsh and grating sound,
Like croak of frog in marshy ground.

" Bury the corpse for midnight's nigh,"
A chaunt of voices seems to sigh ;
" Nay, now I bear my young wife home,
" Come Sexton to the wedding come ;
" Come Priest and bless my lovely bride,
" Ere I dare place her by my side."

The chaunt was hushed, the moon shone clear,
Vanished the crew, the coffin, bier,
Obedient to the rider's call,
Hoorah ! hoorah ! they followed all.
The steed he bounds with snort and stamp,
His hoofs re-echoing tramp, tramp, tramp,
While sparks they scatter, pebbles throw,
As at wild gallop still they go.

Trees and hedges seem to fly,
Right and left as they pass them by ;
Towns and vilages left behind,
Flit like sere leaves on the wind.
" Fears't thou, my love ? the dead ride fast,
" We shall reach the goal of our race at last.
" Fears't thou the dead, my love," he said—
"Oh! let them rest them, rest the dead."

See there ! See there ! round a Judgment throne,
An airy crew seem to dance and crone.
" Come follow us, follow us, my liege men,
" Dance at our wedding my merry men ;
" We speed to our bridal, the guests they wait,
" Join us betimes at the church yard gate."

So the Spirits came hustling fast behind,
As the leaves sweep rustling on the wind,
And still the wild gallop, with snort and stamp,
The steed's hoofs thundering tramp, tramp, tramp,
They scatter the sparks and pebbles throw,
As at mad gallop wild they go.

Still they speed and they speed away,
Like the stars by night and the sun by day.

" Fears't thou, my love? the dead ride fast.

" We shall reach our bridal couch at last.

" Fears't thou the dead?"   " Alas," she said.

   Why wilt thou speak of the silent dead?"

" Hark! hark! I hear the cock doth crow,

" Soon will my flickering sand outflow;

" I smell the scent of the morning air,

" Our course is run, the goal is there.

" Speed, speed, good steed, and thou, my bride,

" Quickly shall sleep by thy lover's side;

" Hoorah! hoorah! the dead ride fast,

" We've reached the place of our rest at last!"

On they rush to a grated door,

Bolt and bar gave way before:

The gates spontaneous open fly,

With clang and jar as the steed draws nigh,

Thro' churchyard drear, over graves they steer,

On many a tomb the moon shines clear.

But, hist! oh, hist! from the knight there fall,

Helmet and armour, and garments all,

In strips like tinder dry they fall.

His scalp is white, without flesh or hair,

His body is naught but a skeleton bare;

And in his hand he holds a glass,
To mark the hours as they swiftly pass,
And over his shoulder a sickle dread,
His harvest to reap of the ghastly dead.

The black steed rears and snuffs the wind,
And snorting scatters sparks behind,
The earth beneath them sinks: the air
Echoes with howls of wild despair;
Low moanings rise up from below,
Down, down into the depths they go.
Maiden, for thee no nuptial wreath,
Alas! thou art the bride of death.

And now in moonlight, round and round,
The spirits in a circle bound,
And howl their joy and ecstasy,
That thus a human soul should die—
" Alas! if God seems hard with thee,
" Strive not, but suffer patiently,
" And thou, poor child, who bravedst Heaven,
" Be thy presumptuous sin forgiven!"

BÜRGER.

Rudolph of Hapsburg.

—◦⁘◦—

At his Coronation banquet,
  In imperial pride elate,
Rudolph, Count of Hapsburg, sat
  Lord of the Palatinate.
The meats with which his table groaned
  Were from the banks of Rhine,
Bohemian vineyards grew the grapes,
  Which sparkled in his wine;
And round him, as the stars of Heaven,
  Surround the glorious sun,
The Seven Electors seated there,
  Did homage every one,
In royal hall, in gorgeous state,
  With banners rich unfurled.
Supporting in his proud estate,
  The Emperor of the World.

Princes and Counts and noble dames
Studded the galleries,
And martial band and trumpet blast
Mixed with the people's cries :
For long a prey to lawless rule,
The poor and weak opprest,
Hailed with acclaim their new found King,
Their rising fortunes blest.
The golden goblet to his lips
The mighty Monarch raised,
And on the glittering scene around,
With smiles complacent gazed.
" Right royal is the sight," he said,
" Right royal the repast ;
" It glads my heart, and pays the debt,
" Of many a sorrow past.
" One feature lacks, and only one,
" In this imperial hall,
" The Bard and Minstrel whom I loved,
" And honored above all :
" As Knight, his counsels won my love,
" His music stole my heart,
" Nor can I now, as Emperor,
" With such companion part."
Then from the crowd an aged man
Stepped forth and bent him low.

E

Stately his form, in flowing robe,
    His locks as white as snow :
Strains of immortal melody,
    Like music of the spheres,
Lay sleeping in his harp and voice,
    Too sweet for mortal ears.
He sang of love and noble deeds,
    With elevating fire,
And charmed his hearers' hearts and bade
    To higher aims aspire.
" Most puissant Emperor," he said,
    " I greet thee loyally,
" At this thy royal banquet ; say,
    " What would'st thou, Sire, with me ?"
" Nay," said the Monarch, " 'Tis not mine,
    " The minstrel to command,
" He serves a mightier Lord than me,
    " Tho' ruler of this land.
" The minstrels gifts are not of earth,
    " 'Tis Heaven inspires his lay,
" The chords that vibrate in his song,
    " Are like the Zephyr's play,
" Or like the muttering of the storm,
    " The tempest's angry roll,
" That come we know not whence,
    " But reach from Pole to Pole :

" And as the fountain from below,
     " In earth's recesses wells,
" And rising from the caverned depths,
     " Into a torrent swells,
" So music's power divinely born,
     " Yields not to man's control,
" But stirs the heart and brings to light,
     " The secrets of the soul."
Then thus adjured the Minstrel struck
     His silver sounding lyre,
And thus he improvised his lay,
     With all a poet's fire :—

Forth to the chase on gallant steed,
     A noble Count was bound,
He crossed the mountain and the mead,
     And heard the torrent's sound.

He neared its banks—a tinkling bell,
     Mixed with the waters roar,
He saw a Priest, and augured well,
     To the sick the Host he bore.

The torrent roared, the torrent roared,
     The Priest he bore the Cross,
The Count knelt down upon the sward,
     Alighting from his horse.

Uncovered, by the raging flood,
    Reverent he bent his head,
For well he knew how Jesus' blood,
    For mortal sins was shed.

The Priest he laid his burthen down,
    He placed it on the grass,
He doffed his shoes and russet gown,
    That he the stream might pass.

The Count with wonder marked the deed,
    " Brav'st thou, Sir Priest, the flood ? "
" Count ! to a dying man I speed,
    " Who pines for heavenly food.

" The trunk that bridged the narrow stream,
    " The floods have borne away,
" And thro' the foaming waves I deem,
    " To wade as best I may."

" Now, God forbid, that thou should'st tread,
    " With such a priceless freight,
" Barefoot the river's stony bed,
    " While I ride thro' in state."

He placed the Priest upon his steed,
    Caparisoned with gold,
And bade him on his errand speed,
    Thro' the waters dark and cold.

" Give me thy steed, Sir Squire," he said,
    Then to the Chase he rode,
The Priest beside the sick man prayed,
    Long in his mean abode.

With morn the noble steed he led,
    (Himself he would not ride),
To where an oak its branches spread
    The postern gate beside.

" Now, Heaven forfend," the Count began,
    " A steed the Host that bore,
" Should e'er be used by mortal man,
    " For chase or battle more.

" Father, I dedicate him now,
    " To pious use for ever,
" For Him to whom my all I owe,
    " Who will forsake me never."

" Count," said the Priest, " Thy words are true,
    " Heaven is a constant friend ;
" Who honors God, He honors too,
    " Blessings his course attend.

" And thou art great for deeds renowned,
    " Six daughters fair are thine,
" Each shall with diadem be crowned,
    " And found a royal line."

With thoughtful mien the Monarch sat,
  Throughout the Minstrel's lay,
In distant times, in distant scenes,
  His thoughts were far away,
But when the music ceased, his mind
  Woke from its dreamy trance,
And when he raised his downcast eyes,
  And caught the minstrel's glance,
The chord was struck, and memories rose,
  Like fountains from below,
He knew the Bard before him there,
  The Priest of long ago,
And hid his falling tears beneath
  His mantle's purple fold,
While all beheld in him the Count
  Of whom the tale was told.

         SCHILLER

Old Moorish Ballad.

———◦◦►◄◦◦———

From Merida a Palmer came,
      Barefoot and meanly drest,
Yet worth the ransom of a king
      Beneath he wore a vest.
To Paris lay his toilsome road,
      And weary and footsore,
He sought no hostel, but repaired
      Straight to the palace door.
" I come to greet His Majesty,
      " I come from far, Sir Page ;"
The page looks at him wonderingly,
      Strange thoughts his mind engage.
" The King at Holy Mass assists,
      " Sir Pilgrim, at the fane,
" Of Him, the holiest of Saints,
      " St. John the Laterane.

" There the Archbishop offers mass,

    " The Cardinal doth preach,

" And happy, whom assembled there,

    " His Eminence doth teach."

The Palmer hastened to the church,

    And kneels him down in prayer

To God, and to his Lady prays,

    In meek devotion there.

Then to the Church his homage pays,

    And to the Imperial Crown,

And to the twelve, who at the board,

    The royal board sit down.

Oliveiros and Orlandos,

    These he honours not,

For they left their royal nephew,

    To a captive's weary lot,

When the Moor had overthrown him,

    On the battle plain,

And they might have rescued him,

    And brought him back again.

Then they rushed upon the Palmer,

    Sword in hand they rushed,

But he raised his staff, and frowning,

    Their fierce anger crushed.

" Peace, Oliveiros," said the King,

    " Orlando, cease thy rage,

" The Pilgrim's mad, or else he boasts
  " A royal lineage."
The Monarch took the Pilgrim's hand,
  " When did'st thou cross the sea ? "
" Sire, in the month of May I passed,
  " Some Moors they captured me.
" They bore me to the Infanta fair,
  " She gave to me her heart,
" She shared her all with me, for long
  " I could not thence depart."
" Nay, Pilgrim," said the King, " in sooth,
  " To such an honoured guest,
" Nursed in the lap of luxury,
  " Captivity is blest."
" Sire," said the Pilgrim, " Merida,
  " Three hundred castles strong,
" And many a Moorish knight defend,
  " From capture and from wrong."
" Thou liest, Sir Pilgrim, foully liest,"
  " Proud Oliveiros cried,
" Not ninety forts protect the place,
  " And not one leader tried."
The Palmer raised his hand to strike—
  To strike the noble knight !
The Monarch with a look severe,
  Prohibited the fight.

F

" Sir Pilgrim, thou art traitor found,

    " Death is thy worthy fate ;

" Thy crimes upon a scaffold high,

    " Now shalt thou expiate ! "

The Pilgrim on the scaffold stood,

    The Monarch stood beside :

" Sir King thou dost me grievous wrong,

    " Woe will thy heart betide,

" One only Son thou hast, and him,

    " Guiltless, thou doom'st to die."

The Empress from her window heard,

    And hastily drew nigh ;

" Sir Pilgrim thou art wan and worn,

    " No mother might thee know,

" But an thou claim'st to be my son,

    " Thy side I prithee show."—

They stripped the rags from off his back,

    And on his shoulder bare,

Beneath the vest of priceless worth,

    The mark they found it there !

Then joy pervades the multitude,

    And plaudits rend the sky,

For France has found the long lost heir,

    And every heart beats high.

The Diver.

The coast was rugged with huge rocks, and deep the waters rolled,
At the precipice's base a promontory bold ;
A storm was raging out at sea—the waves as they recoiled
In surf and foam from the wall below, as in a cauldron boiled.
The King attended by his Court stood on the rude plateau,
And gazed in horror and amaze on the seething mass below.
Then turning to his knights he said, " This golden cup is his,
" Who'll pierce the billow's foaming crest, and snatch it from the abyss !"
The knights looked grave, the knights looked cold, while thrice the Monarch
    spoke;
At last the courtiers' crowded ranks a graceful stripling broke,
He threw his cloak upon the ground, and with an inward prayer,
He cast him from the giant rock and cut the nether air,
Like bolt from Heaven he struck the wave, like shaft from bended bow,
A moment in the foam he glanced, then disappeared below.
The waters boiled, the waters seethed, the tempest wailing howled,
And Heaven above, with omen dark, in lurid blackness scowled.

Breathless the mute spectators gazed, from the promontory steep.
No sight was seen, no voice was heard, no message from the deep,
But what is that which like a speck upon the mountain's side,
Exuding from the watery waste, breasts buoyantly the tide ?
'Tis he! though boiling surges toss, the billows bear him up,
His foot is on the solid rock, he clasps the golden cup!
One look to Heaven, one glance around, the noble stripling threw,
And on a maiden's cheek there came a blush of roseate hue.
" Sir King," he said," " in the caverns green, where the mermaids hold their
    court,
" And the ravening monsters of the deep to seek their prey resort;
" I held my way till the cup I saw—on a coral reef it shone,
" I seized it, and behold it here, thy dangerous quest is done !"
A murmur of approval rose, " Sir Youth," the Monarch said,
" Brave is thy heart and strong thy hand, the quest is nobly sped ;
" See you this ring and her who wears—you worship at her shrine—
" Bring me that gem from the depths below, and maid and gem are thine !"
The youth his cheek a moment paled, the maid looked marble cold,
A glance to Heaven, a glance to her, their secret passion told—
The waters boiled, the waters seethed, the tempest wailing howled,
And Heaven above, with omen dark, in lurid blackness scowled,
He plunged into the depths below, the waves above him close,
They gazed for long, they gazed in vain, no more the stripling rose !

SCHILLER.

The Dragon.

———⊸⋅⟩⟨⟨⟨∘∘————

The crowds collect, the people shout,
The streets are full of rabble rout.
Ye Gods! what means this tumult dire;
Are all gone mad? Is Rhodes on fire?
I see a knight encased in mail,
A dragon at his horse's tail,
With serpent fold, and looks of guile,
And gaping jaws, like crocodile,
What wonder that the people gaze,
At knight and monster with amaze!

And hark! a thousand tongues exclaim,
" Behold the knight of peerless fame,
" The slayer of the dragon bold,
" Terror of peasant, byre and fold.

" Many a knight went forth before.

" But none in life returnèd more !

" All honour to the noble knight,

" Who braved and won the desperate fight ! "

Thus, as they spoke, the crowds drew nigh

St. John the Baptist's Monastry,

Where all the knights assembled sate

In conclave on affairs of state.

The youthful knight presents him there.

Before the proud Grand Master's chair ;

The people crowd the galleries,

With wild enthusiastic cries,

But not a sound the silence breaks,

When thus the noble stripling speaks :

" Of Holy Church, unworthy Son.

" My knightly duty I have done,

" The Dragon, terror of the land,

" Lies there the victim of my hand !

" The peasant now may reap and sow,

" The traveller on his journey go,

" The pilgrim visit at the shrine,

" Where mercy dwells and grace divine."

Then spake the Prince in accents low,

" Sir Knight, thy prowess I allow ;

" And valour is a virtue bright,

" That well becomes a belted knight,

" But he who wields our Order's sword,

" And bears the Cross of Christ, our Lord,

" What is the first and great command,

" That rules his actions, guides his hand ?'

Then all were silent—but the youth,

Ingenuous and full of truth,

Replied, " Obedience is the test,

" Of worthiness the first, the best."

" Son," said the Prince, with aspect cold,

" This first great law, thou'st broken bold,

" Presumptuous, drawn thy falchion's blade,

" When our great Order's rules forbade."

With mien composed, the youth replied,

" Not boldly I the law defied ;

" Unwittingly I deemed that I

" Did with its Spirit, Prince, comply,

" When forth I issued, sword in hand,

" To drive a monster from the land

" Five of our Order, peerless knights,

" Crowned victors in a hundred fights,

" Had on this fatal errand bled,

" Since by thy word prohibited ;

" Long did my mind on vengeance brood,

" And ever in my dreams I stood,

" With this dread monster, face to face,

" And when my waking thoughts had place,

" I listened to the morning's tale

" Of slaughter fresh, with visage pale,

" And vengeful schemes did over ride

" My every sense and thought beside.

" Then in my heart the passion grew,

" What ancient heroes dared to do,

" Impetuous acts the cold may scan,

" 'Tis youthful deeds adorn the man.

" The knights of old their country cleared

" Of plagues and monsters to be feared,

" The lion and the minotaur,

" The dragon and a thousand more.

" When wrong and rapine walked the earth,

" They deemed their blood but little worth.

" Is now the Saracen alone,

" A fitting foe for valour grown ?

" Must not the servant of the Lord,

" In any quarrel draw his sword,

" Where human wrongs can be redrest,

" To help the injured and opprest ?

" And then I deemed that art and guile
" Must supplement my strength the while,
" That skill and forethought might prevail
" Where courage only well might fail.

" Then sudden to my mind occurred
" A thought, to thee I gave it word.
" Grand Master! to my heart has come,
" A fond desire to see my home.
" Most graciously, thou heard'st my tale,
" I crossed the sea with flowing sail ;
" Soon did I reach my native shore,
" I trod its well-known haunts once more,
" And art employed to fabricate,
" The hideous Dragon's fitting mate.

" Its aspect worked a deadly spell—
" Its mouth was like the gates of Hell,
" The teeth that armed its gaping jaw,
" Were like the ridges of a saw ;
" The tongue as sharp as rapier blade,
" The eyes like forkèd lightning played,
" And from his scaly back out rolled
" A coil might man and beast enfold.

" Part Dragon foul, the workman's art
" Had made him, salamander part,

G

" A creature, awful to behold,

" When on the sand his length was rolled.

" Two bloodhounds next, both fierce and fleet,

" I taught to follow at my feet,

" And hounded on their native rage

" The hideous monster to engage,

" While mounted on my Arab steed,

" I spurred him on to daring deed,

" And fiercely charged the monster dread,

" Hurling my javelin at his head.

" At first my horse in terror reared,

" And plunged and foamed in horror weird,

" My dogs recoiled with mute affright,

" Yet still I urged them to the fight.

" Thus for three months, with patient care,

" I trained and exercised them there ;

" And when I thought them well prepared,

" Straight to the vessel I repaired—

" The third day saw us disembark,

" And ready for the exploit dark.

" With feelings deep my heart was moved,

" Of pity for the land I loved.

" I found the peasants in despair,

" The shepherds gone, the pastures bare,

" I cheered the serfs as best I might,

" With prospects of the coming fight,

" And mounted on my charger fleet,

" The bloodhounds following at my feet,

" I sought the secret hiding place,

" Where lurked the terror of our race.

" Master, thou know'st the humble shrine,

" Built on a rock, for use divine—

" There on the altar, meek and mild,

" Preside the Mother and the Child,

" The Pilgrim wan, who thither wends,

" A hundred weary steps ascends ;

" But when his way-worn feet attain

" The heights that crown the nether plain,

" With holy joy and faith replete,

" He kneels him at the Saviour's feet.

" Beneath it is a grotto dark,

" Damp and obscure with herbage rank,

" Where never enters ray of sun—

" There did the light the monster shun ;

" There, day and night, in ambush lay,

" To scour the country, seize his prey.

" Thus did a fiend of hell reside,

" God's holy altar close beside,

" And Pilgrims to the sacred spot,
" Were seized and mangled in the grot.

" And first the rock I did ascend,
" Then on my knees did lowly bend,
" There pardon asked for all my sin,
" And strength in battle field to win ;
" Then girded on my trusty sword,
" Mounted my horse, and gave the word.
" Scarce had I reached the plain below,
" When loud the bloodhounds barked, and, lo !
" My charger snorting, mad with fear,
" Began to plunge and wildly rear,
" For there the hideous monster lay,
" Coiled like a ball upon the clay.

" At the dread sight the bloodhounds gnash
" Their teeth, and on the monster dash,
" But swift as arrow they recoil,
" In horror from the deadly broil,
" When from his jaws the poisonous breath
" Exhales the atmosphere of death,
" And fearful howlings pierce the air,
" Like cry of jackal from his lair—
" But soon I cheer them on again,
" And hurl my spear with might and main ;

" Rebounding from its armed scales,

" Harmless as reed the weapon fails.

" And now my horse in wild affright,

" Defies control and rears upright,

" And then methought my end was nigh,

" I breathed a prayer, I heaved a sigh,

" As open wide and deep I saw,

" The hideous monster's armed jaw.

" An instant on the ground I stand,

" Beside the monster, sword in hand,

" But vain are all attempts t'assail,

" The scaly dragon's coat of mail.

" Enraged he strikes me with his tail,

" And prostrate on the ground I lie,

" His yawning jaws before me spy,

" The gnashing of his teeth I hear,

" All vain are then or sword or spear,

" But haply at the moment turning,

" My dogs with savage fury burning,

" Dashed at his flanks, and with a cry,

" The monster turned in agony.

" Then to my feet I quickly rose,

" His struggles fierce his maw expose,

" Then in his heart I buried there,

" With fatal stroke my weapon bare,

" In mighty stream the black blood flows,
" The monster sinks in deadly throes,
" Beneath his lifeless form I lie,
" Exhausted there I seem to die ;
" And when I wake my train surround
" The Dragon weltering on the ground."

The youth was still, his tale was told—
Rivers of pent up feeling rolled
Over the surging masses there ;
A thousand plaudits rent the air !
Amazement, joy, and gratitude,
Inspired the excited multitude !
The Brothers of the Order claim
To crown the Knight with wreath of fame ;
The people burn to do him grace,
As Saviour of the human race—
But cold and stern, with bearing proud,
The Prince bids silence in the crowd.

And thus he speaks, " Most noble youth,
" Valiant art thou, my son, in truth—
" The terror of this peaceful land
" Has fallen a victim to thy hand—
" In thee a God the people know,
" To *us* thou com'st a deadly foe,

" For in thy heart there lurks a curse
" To this our Holy Order worse,
" Than to this land the monster fierce,
" Whom thou with fatal steel did'st pierce—
" The serpent, deadliest to mankind,
" The ruin of his soul and mind,
" Is disobedience and self will ;
" Parents of every human ill,
" They reign, the ruin and the curse
" Of man and of the universe !

" Valour the Mameluke may claim,
" Submission is the Christian's aim,
" Hence where our blessed Lord has trod,
" Our Holy Order worships God,
" And here to tame our rampant will,
" Our highest duty we fulfil—
" Thee love of fame has led astray,
" Thou in our Order must not stay,
" Who shuns his sacred yoke to bear,
" Christ's holy Cross may never wear."

Into wild tumult breaks the crowd,
The hall resounds with murmurs loud,
The youth alone, with downcast eye,
Meekly his Order's garb lays by,

Salutes the Master with a sigh,
And turns.   But on the Master's face
Stern coldness quick to love gives place.
He calls him back with tearful eyes,
" Embrace me, oh ! my Son," he cries,
" Well hast thou fought a battle sore,
" Our Order's symbol take once more,
" Thy patience has redeemed thy loss,
" Humility deserves the Cross !"

SCHILLER.

Fridolin.

A loyal youth was Fridolin,
    To God and to his lady true,
To do her will, her smile to win.
    Was all the joy on earth he knew.

The lovely Countess of Taverne,
    Her every art and whim he knew,
Each thought untold he could discern,
    And loved her as a page might do.

The huntsman Kunigund beheld,
    And hate and malice filled his breast,
His heart with angry passions swelled,
    And jealous envy marred his rest.

Then home returning from the chase,
    He arms his tongue with artful guile,
And schemes to give suspicion place,
    In the fond husband's breast the while.

" How blest art thou, Sir Count," he says,
    " Blest in thy fair and youthful bride,
" And him who such fond homage pays,
    " And ever wanders by her side."

" What mean'st thou, knave ? " with furious rage,
    The Count exclaims, with flashing eyes—
" Nay, Count, I speak but of the page,"
    The wary huntsman cold replies.

Furious the Count his courser spurs,
    Thro' devious ways, mid brakes and briars,
To where a forest, dark with firs,
    Gleams with the smelting furnace fires.

Here day and night the bellows roar,
    And swarthy gangs the furnace feed,
Till hissing flows the molten ore,
    And fiery streams like lava speed.

Two serfs he summons of the band—
    " When here there comes a man to learn,

" If ye have done your lord's command,
    " Then cast him in yon hell to burn."

Now Kunigund full courteously,
    Accosts the page with hidden hate,
" Comrade, the Count would speak with thee,
    " He waits thee by the postern gate."

" Page," said the Count, with downcast air,
    " Go hie thee, seek the smelter band,
" And ask the serfs assembled there,
    " Have they fulfilled their lord's command ? "

" Thy bidding, Count, I haste to do "—
    So spoke the page,—but ere he went,
Swift to his lady's side he flew,
    And there with low obeisance bent.

" Lady," he said, " afield I go,
    " To do the bidding of my lord,
" Yet ere I go, fain would I know,
    " If thou for me hast wish or word."

Then spake the lady of Taverne
    In accents musically mild,
" To hear a holy mass I yearn,
    " But dare not leave my ailing child.

" Go, youth, and say for me a prayer,
    " Kneeling before St. Hilda's shrine,
" And when thy sins thou weepest there,
    " May I alike find grace for mine."

Then, happy in his welcome task,
    He follows where the belfry chimes
With solemn tones the sinner ask
    To seek forgiveness for his crimes.

" Oh ! never turn thee from thy God,
    " Whene'er he meets thee in the way ! "—
Slowly the sacred aisles he trod,
    And humbly knelt him down to pray.

" Not lost the minutes given to prayer,"
    He murmurs, and devoutly bends,
Till mass is said, and service there
    With priestly benediction ends.

Then forth he goes, with conscience light,
    Thro' rocks and woods by devious ways.
To where the smelting fires burn bright,
    And there twelve paternosters says.

And now the furnace mouth before,
    He sees the swarthy laborers stand.

And shouts above the bellows roar,
  " Serfs, have ye done your lord's command ? "

Grim at the forkéd flames they gaze,
  Grimly they smile, the savage band,—
" Our lord award us well earned praise,
  " Duly we've done his stern command."

Swift with his message speeds the youth,
  The Count amazed beholds him run,
And doubts the voice, nor deems it truth
  Which says, " Sir Count, thy bidding's done."

" Unhappy youth, whence com'st thou, say ? "—
  " Straight from the forge I come, my Lord."—
" Say, hast thou loitered on the way,
  " That thus thou bring'st such tardy word."

" Sir Count, my lady bade me kneel,
  " At Hilda's shrine in lowly prayer,
" For thine and for her spirit's weal—
  " Duly I told my rosary there."

The Count with terror viewed the lad,
  " What message bring'st thou from the band ? "
" Sir Count, with air severe and sad,
  " They said, ' they'd done their Lord's command.' "

" And what of Kunigund, I pray ? "
    Trembling, he questioned eagerly.
" Did'st thou not meet him by the way ?
    " I bade him haste to follow thee."

" Naught saw I of him, sooth, my lord,
    " In pasture green or forest dun."—
" Then God has judged him, by my word,
    " So may His holy will be done."

And kindly, as was *not* his wont,
    He took the stripling by the hand,
And led him to the terrace front,
    Where lone he saw the Countess stand.

" Lady," he said, " Behold this youth,
    " Full foully has he been maligned ;
" But God has proved his worth and truth,
    " Be thou to him as ever kind."

               SCHILLER.

The Wild Huntsman.

On Rhine's fair banks 'tis a festal morn,
The Baron von Falsberg blows his horn.
Halloo! halloo! to the chase it sounds,
Neighing and prancing, his fleet steed bounds;
His train of attendants follow pell mell,
While the pack from their kennel yelp and yell,
As they dash thro' cornfield, brake and dell.

The sabbath morning's sunbeam's gilt
The dome for holy worship built,
The bell with solemn tone invites,
Hollow and clear to the sacred rites,
While many a hymn of praise and prayer
From many a choir is borne on air.

Over the crossway swift they go,
With whoop! halloo! and tally ho!
And see you, and see you, on either side
Of the huntsman bold two horsemen ride,
The steed on the right is like silver white,
The steed on the left as furnace bright.

Who are these horsemen to left and right?
Full well I guess, but I may not write.
The knight on the right is sublimely grand,
With his mild sweet face, and aspect bland,
The knight on the left is malign and stern,
And his eyes like red hot charcoal burn.

"Welcome!" said he, of the evil face,
"Welcome! sir Knight, to the noble chase,
"In earth or heaven can nought compare,
"With sport like this, on day so fair."
And as he spoke, he slapped his thigh,
And jauntingly waved his cap on high.

"Sir Count," said he of the gracious mien,
"Ill sounds thy horn on this morn serene,
"Trust me no good can those betide,
"Who on this holy day do ride.
"Be warned by thy angel good—return;
"The counsels dark of the evil one spurn."

" To the chase, Sir Count, forth away to the chase,"
Said he of the dark ill-favored face,
" What a chime of bells, what jocund sounds
" With blast of horn and yelp of hounds,
" And whoop, halloo, and hark away!—
" I'll show you glorious sport to-day."

" Well hast thou spoken thou left man kind,
" Thou art a Hero after my mind,
" He who cares nought for the noble chase,
" May say paternosters and pray for grace,—
" Saint on my right, thou pleadest in vain,
" I hie to the hunting grounds amain."

And Hurrah ! Hurrah ! on, on they speed,
Up hill, down dale, over crops and mead,
And ever at the Baron's side,
To right and left, the two Knights ride,—
When sudden with antler's branching high,
A milk white stag comes bounding by.

Whoop ! whoop ! halloo ! the horns blow shrill,
Down thro' the valley and over the hill,
When, lo, from the train behind and before,
One drops down, and is trampled o'er,
" Leave them to die, to hell let them go,
" Never knight's sport was mar-red so."

I

The wild deer crouched in the standing wheat,
Deeming it's cover a safe retreat,
On came the field, huntsmen and pack,
A peasant stepped forth, and waved them back,
" Have pity my Lord, have pity and spare,
" The poor man's hard earned pittance bare."

The Knight on the right then swift up-rode,
And gently urged his counsels good,
But he on the left with the evil eye,
Encouraged the Count maliciously,
And again the right Knight's warnings fail,
Again the left Knight's word's prevail.

"Out of my sight, hound, out of my way"!
Hear the Count to the poor man say,
" Away, away, or I'll ride thee down,
" Thy corpse shall be to my bloodhounds thrown ;
" Ho, ho, my men, go seize him there,
" And lay your whips on his shoulders bare."

He spoke, 'twas done, the Madman dashed
Over hedges and gates, thro' rivers plashed,
The train they run, and they ride pell mell,
Huntsmen, horses and hounds as well,
And with hoof and foot, they crush and pound
The blades of corn on the ruined ground.

Herds of deer by the noise alarmed,
Hie from their coverts like spirits charmed,
And panting, dash with headlong speed
Thro' brake and briar to a grassy mead,
Where browsing herds of cattle tame,
Seem refuge for the wilder game.

But hither and thither thro' wood and dell,
Hither and thither thro' dell and wood,
Halloo ! halloo ! with yelp and yell,
The hounds and huntsmen rush like a flood;
The shepherd trembling for his herd,
Falls on his knees before his lord.

" Mercy ! my lord, mercy, I pray !
" Call off your dogs, forbear to slay
" These harmless flocks and herds this day,
" See, in these inmates of the stall,
" The widows and the orphans' all.
" Have pity on the poor and spare
" Their harmless browsing beasts to tear."

Again the Knight on the right uprode,
And gently urged his counsels good,
But he, on the left, with the evil eye,
Encouraged the Count maliciously,

And again the right Knight's warnings fail,
Again the left Knight's words prevail.

" Out of my way, audacious hound,
" Would that thy shapeless limbs were bound,
" Thy sleekest, fattest beast around;
" Glad should I be to see thee driven,
" With all thy lowing herd to Heav'n."

" On, on, my men! on, on, my pack!"
The hounds come following on the track.
Each seizes the nearest for his prey,
The hills resound with the wild affray,
The herdsman welters in his gore,
The browsing herd exists no more.

The milk white stag eludes the fray,
And through the forest takes its way,
With slackened speed and drooping neck,
His sleek skin bossed with crimson fleck,
And plunging deep into the dell,
Takes refuge in a hermit's cell.

Still on the hounds and huntsman go,
With crack of whip and tally-ho!
With blast of horn, and bark, and yell,
The wild swarm gallop through the dell.

When forth to meet, with gown and hood,
Behold! the Hermit of the Wood.

" Cease, cease, from this unholy chase,
" Nor dare to desecrate this place,
" To Heaven these slaughtered victims cry,
" For wrath on those who Heaven defy,
" Be warned, ye wicked men in time,
" Or Heaven will punish sore your crime."

Once more the Knight on the right uprode,
And gently urged his counsel's good,
But he on the left with the evil eye
Encouraged the Count maliciously.
And again the right Knight's warnings fail,
Again the left Knight's words prevail.

" Ruin here, or ruin there,
" 'Tis naught to me, what do I care ?
" Though thrice a Heaven or Hell were there.
" There's not a bat that I would spare,
" Displease it God, displease it thee,
" Enough, thou fool, it pleaseth me ! "

He cracked his whip, his horn he blew,
" Onward, my comrades, brave and true ! "

But, ah ! both Monk and hut are gone,
Horses and men alike have flown ;
A stillness, as of death, succeeds
The crash of hunters, hounds, and steeds.

The Count looks round, and o'er and o'er,
He blows his horn—it sounds no more—
He shouts !—no echoes reach his ears,—
He cracks his whip !—no noise he hears !—
He plies his horse with whip and spur,
Forward nor backward will he stir !

Dark as the grave is all around,
Till issuing hollow from the ground,
A voice like ocean's sullen roar,
Breaking upon a rocky shore,
Or thunder rumbling over head,
Denounces loud, Heaven's sentence dread.

" Thou tyrant, demon of thy race !
" In earth, or Heaven, unworthy place !
" The voice of tortured creatures cries
" For justice to the outraged skies,
" Where Vengeance rears her flaming torch,
" And summons to the judgment porch.

" Fly, monster, fly ! and know that ne'er
" Shall aught arrest thy wild career
" While time endures.   A fatal spell
" Shall see thee chased by fiends from Hell ;
" Warning to Princes for all time.
" Who outrage Heaven and earth by crime."

And now a sulphurous atmosphere,
Floats o'er the forest like a bier,—
His breath is laboured—eyesight dim—
Agony shoots through marrow and limb,
Behind is sound of tempest's roar,
The blast of horror lies before.

The hurricane roars with poisonous breath,
The forest is black as the jaws of death,
When out of the night a colossal wrist,
Looms in the air with clench-ed fist—
It opens, it clutches, and see ! his face
Is turned behind to the demon chase.

Around are flames of every hue,
Fires like a furnace,— red, green, and blue,
Billows of flame, like ocean's swell,
Peopled by floating broods of Hell,
And a thousand curs from the depths below,
Through the blazing forest howling go.

Mad with affright he scours the plain,
Shrieking and yelling with fear and pain,
Ever and ever, through the wide world,
Hell bellows after him as he is whirled,
By day through clefts in the mountain bare,
By night on the blast of the murky air.

Ever his head behind is turned,
Swift or slow, as the ground is spurned,
Tracked by the bloodhounds of Hell he sees,
The fangs that would snap, and the jaws would seize,
And anguish and terror rend his heart,
As his blood-shot eyes from their sockets start.

Such the Wild Huntsman's fearful chase,—
A ceaseless, never-ending race,
Till the dread day of judgment come—
For him no rest, and for him no home !
And ever, as in the dead of night
    The hellish crew sweep howling by.
The kindred wretch starts up with fright,
    At sound of the weird, unearthly cry !

BÜRGER.

The Glove.

King Francis sat on his blazoned throne, attended by his Court,
And dames and knights assembled there to see the royal sport,
Around the amphitheatre, in ranges tier on tier,
A thousand mute spectators sat, till the victims should appear—
The Monarch gave the signal dread, the signal to begin
The games where some a cruel death, and some should glory win.
Then opened wide an iron door in the prison's under ground,
And forth a stately lion stalked, and proudly gazed around—
Then listless, yawning, shook himself, and idly laid him down,
Right royal in his attitude, as though he bore a crown.
Once more the Monarch gave the sign and from an open door,
A royal tiger sudden sprang, and bounded on the floor ;
Then lashed his tail and savage growled as his ancient foe he spied,
And circling round the crouching beast, he laid him by his side—
Again the Monarch gave the sign, again the portal yawns,
And from the dark recesses spring two leopards fleet as fawns.

K

Thirsting for blood they dash upon the tiger with their claws,
Eager for fight he threatens them, with wide extended jaws.
Then from the ground the king of beasts uprears his stately form,
And silence in the arena reigns—a lull before the storm—
But sudden from the gallery, where beauteous forms abound,
A glove, of daintiest symmetry, falls fluttering to the ground,
Between the royal beasts it 'lights, a gage of battle there,
And a voice like music soft is heard to cleave the liquid air—
" Sir Heinrich, if thy vows are true, and for my love thou carest,
" Go, fetch me from the wild beasts' den my gauntlet if thou darest !"
Then swift descends the knight and soon, the royal beasts between,
To lords' and ladies' wonderment, his noble form is seen.
With check unblanched, and steady hand, he raises up the glove.
Then mounting to the gallery he bears it to his love—
The lady smiled approval sweet, the knight he turned away,
" I care not for your thanks, fair dame, nor for your favors stay !"

SCHILLER.

Rechberg.

———⌒⋆⋇∘⊙———

Rechberg was a reckless youth,
    Tho' knightly spurs he wore,
He was a highwayman in truth,
    And robbed the Merchant's store.

One night he ambushed in a Church,
    A caravan to seize,
When night should leave them in the lurch,
    Among the forest trees.

He mounted in the midnight gloom,
    But far he had not gone,
" I've left my gloves " he said " Sir Groom,
    Upon the cold tombstone."

The youth returns pale with affright—
　　" Your gloves the devil take.
" A ghost sits on the tomb, Sir Knight,
　　"My limbs with terror quake.

" The ghost he put your gauntlets on,
　　" With eyes of fire he gazed,
" He stroked them up, and stroked them down,
　　" My sight with fear was dazed."

The knight rides back, in haste rides back,
　　And bold confronts the ghost,
The ghost succumbs to his attack,
　　And cedes the gloves he'd lost.

Then speaks the ghost in accents drear,
　　" An the gloves thou cans't not spare,
" Yet lend them me for one short year,
　　" The nice close fitting pair."

" To prove the devil's faith and truth,
　　" The gloves to thee I'll lend,
" Upon thy shrivelled paws in sooth,
　　" They will not burst or rend."

Rechberg mounts quick—and off has rode,
　　And thro' the forest spurred,

Already chanticleer has crowed,
    When tramp of horse is heard.

A knightly cavalcade rides past,
    In masks, a dark array,
The youth draws back, his heart beats fast
    As on they take their way.

A Squire behind the solemn train,
    A coal black charger led,
Caparizoned with sell and rein,
    And trappings of the dead.

Rechberg steps forth from his ambuscade,
    " Sir Squire, my riddle read,
" Whose is this stately cavalcade ?
    " And whose this coal black steed."?

" The steed belongs to a servant true,
    " Of my Lord (who rides before)
" Rechberg, well known all the country through,
    " A year—he'll be no more."

The Squire passed on—the wretched youth
    Addrest him to his groom ;
Now take my horse, for here in truth,
    " Alas ! I've heard my doom.

" If not too weighty be this sword,
 " This lance and trusty shield,
" Take them in memory of thy Lord,
 " But in God's service wield."

He wends him to a Convent gate,
 " Lord Abbot let me in,
" As Servant here in low estate,
 " To expiate my sin."

" Thou art a knight—deny it not,
" Thy spurs thy rank proclaim,
" To tend our steeds shall be thy lot,
 " The wild, the young, to tame."

Now the Lord Abbot that day year,
 A wild black steed did buy,
Rechberg the bold, unknowing fear,
 The vicious beast would try.

He plunged, he reared, erect he stood,
 The youth like wild beast tore,
Then disappearing in the wood
 Was never heard of more.

On the youth's grave at midnight cold,
 A groom is seen to alight,

From coal black steed—the stirrup hold,
    And gauntlets gleaming bright.

Then from his grave does Rechberg rise,
    Beneath the cold tombstone,
Mounts—dons his gloves—and flies
    Into the forest lone.

To warn you, youths, this tale is told,
    To keep your gloves in sight,
Nor ride the land, marauders bold,
    But stay at home by night.

                    UHLAND.

The Goldsmith's Daughter.

—◦◦⦂◦⦂◦◦—

A goldsmith gazed with admiring eye,
    On his cases of gems and pearls,
And he said to a maiden standing by,
    With brilliant eyes and golden curls—
" Of all my jewels, so rich and rare,
" Daughter thou art the most precious there."

There entered a knight of noble mien—
    " Welcome, sweet maiden, lovely and true,
" With thy golden locks and thy sparkling een,
    " Welcome, Sir Goldsmith, too !—
" Now make me a wreath that shall be thy pride,
" To encircle the brow of my beautiful bride ! "

The goldsmith wrought, with skill and care,
A wreath that the proudest queen might wear ;

And when it was done, and the maid alone,
　　She gazed, and she whispered tremblingly,
　　" Oh ! would it were made for me !
" How happy the bride that will wear that crown !
　　" That will wear it unto death,—
Oh, would he but give me, that knight, for my own.
　　" Of roses one simple wreath."

Now, see, to the goldsmith's house once more,
　　The knight his footsteps wend,
With a courteous smile he enters the door,
　　" Welcome, sweet maid, and thou, old friend !
" Now make for my lovely bride to wear,
" A ring of jewels most costly and rare."

So when the glittering ring was done,
　　With diamonds and rubies set,
Sweet Helen she gazed on it all alone,
　　Till her smiles grew sad, and her cheeks were wet.
And the brilliants seemed robbing her eyes of light,
As she slipt the ring on her finger slight.

" Oh ! blest is the bride who shall wear this ring,"
　　She murmured tremblingly ;
" Oh ! would he but give me some little thing,
　　" To keep for his sake, how blest should I be,—

L

" A lock of his hair, to lie near my heart,

" A treasure from which I would never part."

Quickly the knight returned again,

  On the costly ring he gazed.

" Sir Goldsmith, be sure that thy skill and thy pain,

  " By my lovely bride shall be praised !—

" Now, maiden, permit me to try upon thee,

" The gifts for my bride—thou art lovely as she ! "

'Twas the morn of the Sabbath, the day of sweet rest,

  Mid the chiming of bells the knight came,

Sweet Helen for church was decked out in her best,

  And she blushed with an innocent shame,

When the knight, with a smile, bowing courteously low,

Placed the ring on her hand and the crown on her brow.

" Now Helen, my sweetest, my bride !

  " Forgive me the innocent jest ;

" For thou art my love and my pride—

  " Without thee my life were unblest !

" 'Twas for thee that the jewels were blended,—

" For thee that the crown was intended !

" Thy lot hath been hitherto cast,

  " Mid the purest, the richest, the rarest,

" Thy future shall be as the past,

   " When with me thy fair fortunes thou sharest,—

" And be sure, my old friend, ere we part,

" Thy jewel I'll wear next my heart ! "

UHLAND.

The Tyrant of Samos.

———⊸⁑⊶———

Upon his tower, the tyrant stood,
    His royal guest beside,
On Samos Isle around he gazed,
    With a countenance of pride.
" Confess " he said to Egypt's King,
    " The Gods espouse my cause,
" Throughout the land the vanquished race
    " Obey their Conqueror's laws."
" Tyrant" the King of Egypt said,
    " Boast not too soon thy power,
" Thy sceptre reigns triumphant now,
    " But who may tell the hour
" When he, whose wrath for vengeance burns
    " Shall hurl thee from thy throne,
" And spoil the spoiler of his crown,
    " And seize it for his own."

Thus, while he spoke, a messenger
    Came riding furiously—
" My liege, thy foe is dead, the war
    Is ended gloriously."
" See now " the Tyrant said, " O King.
    " My triumph is complete "—
" Not so, my friend," the King replied,
    " While danger threats thy fleet."
And as he spoke a message came,
    " Thy fleet at anchor lies
" With store of treasure from the East.
    " And many a noble prize."
Lost in astonishment
    The King of Egypt stood,
But soon his mind resumed
    Its philosophic mood.
" Tyrant, the Cretan fleet is near,
    " Hark to the plashing oars,
" Who speaks of triumph when
    " Invasion threats his shores ? "
But while he spoke the news arrived,
    " A fatal storm has blown,
" The Cretan squadron is dispersed,
    " And all its galleys strewn."
My Friend " the King of Egypt said,
    " Now – much I fear for thee,

" Once was I blest with every gift
  " A mortal could desire—
" I had an only son who lived,
  " The darling of his sire,
" The Gods required a sacrifice,
  " They took my only child ;
" I paid my debt to fortune then,
  " And never since have smiled,
" Woulds't thou be spared a fate as hard,
  " Select thy richest prize,
" The dearest to thine inmost heart,
  " The treasure of thine eyes,
" And cast it into ocean's bed,
  " And with the gift appease,
" The furies jealous hate of man,
  " The Gods immortal please."
The Monarch's words alarmed his friend,
  He took a priceless gem,
Meet for a Sultan's turbaned brow,
  Or royal diadem,
He threw it to the depths below—
  " Ye Gods my offering take,
" Nor in your anger cast me down,
  " Your votary forsake."—
Morn dawned upon the Tyrant's tower,
  A fisherman stood there—

" Accept " he said " Oh King, a fish,

   " Of excellence most rare,

" Ne'er have I caught so rich a prize

   " In all my pilgrimage."

The Tyrant took the gift with thanks,

   And gave it to a page,

The page came running back, " My Liege,

   " Within the fish's maw

" The Chief has found this precious gem

   " A diamond without flaw."

Amazement filled the Tyrant's mind,

   He knew its form and hue,

It was the gem, but yesternight

   Into the waves he threw—

The King with consternation gazed!

   " My friend thy doom is sealed,

" I never knew such fate as this

   " To mortal man revealed—

" I dare no longer be thy friend,

   " No longer stay with thee,

" Lest in one fatal destiny

   " We both included be."

                SCHILLER.

The Chapel in the Wood.

The dark wood girts the grassy downs,
Beyond, the grey hill gloomy frowns ;
The withered leaf, the pattering rain,
Tell us that winter comes amain.

Slow sinks the sun, wrapt in a shroud
Of dark, unsympathizing cloud ;
And nature dumb, in twilight's gloom,
Seems brooding o'er her coming doom.

There where the streamlet ripples by
The leafless oak that soars so high,
An ancient chapel courts the gaze,
Telling a tale of bygone days.

Where are they fled, the goodly throng,
That filled its aisles with pious song?—
Released from this world's weary prison,
They with their songs to Heav'n have risen!

Hark! what harsh cry the stillness mars,—
Upon the affrighted ear it jars!
The unearthly wail, whose sound appals,
Seems issuing from those ruined walls.

Now shouts it praise to God on high,—
Now with mad laughter fills the sky!
Then Hallelujah's shrieks profane,
And then with laughter peals again.

He rushes by at headlong pace,
His white hair streaming from his face,—
A wretch, with eyes like meteors bright,
The wandering stars of madness-night.

Now thro' the wood his footsteps thread,
The sear leaf rustles 'neath his tread;
He stops—He listens—can it be?—
I hear him weeping bitterly.

And now a melancholy light
Dawns on the valley, coldly bright,
The moon looks down with silvery sheen,
On Autumn's last departing scene.

M

Upward the Maniac turns his gaze,
On his wan face the moonbeam plays,—
Lights his pale cheek, and bitter smile,
The chill wind sighing past the while.

Oh, piteous sight! his vacant eye
Turns to the realms of peace on high,
Where in their course the planets roll,
The regions of the parted soul.

What, then, oh! Fate, has this man done,
That thou hast blotted out his Sun ?—
His reason from its throne hast hurled,
And left him Godless in the world ?

He loved—a long sad time ago—
He knew not care, nor dreamt of woe;
With her he loved, those paths he trod,
And in yon chapel worshipped God.

They entered, and knelt down to pray,
With the last sunbeam's slanting ray;
And while the shepherds played without
They bent in common prayer devout.

Then with a solemn voice, and low,
She raised her hand, and vowed her vow,
To love him with eternal truth,
So Heav'n might punish without ruth.

And when his heart responded true,
The sunbeams glowed a warmer hue ;
And from without the melody,
Sounded like music from the sky.

Alas ! how soon his dream of bliss,
Vanished before another's kiss,—
Her broken vows, the perjured bride,
In cold indifference cast aside.

And joy was hers, without remorse,—
No sorrow marred life's flowing course,—
She lived, unpunished by the God,
Whose House of Prayer she perjured trod.

And this is what that man has done,
That Fate has blotted out his Sun,
His reason from its throne has hurled,
And left him Godless in the world.

And hence it is, in withering scorn,
He curses God,—alone, forlorn ;
And like an outcast wanders round,
Those ancient walls so faithless found.

LENAU.

The Bard.

"What sounds of music freight the breeze,
   "Beyond the Castle walls,
"Fain would I welcome strains like these
   "Within these ancient Halls"!
The Monarch spoke, "Page, bid the guard,
"Give entrance to the glorious Bard"

"Greetings, my Lords and Ladies fair,
   "I greet you from afar,
"What galaxy of splendours rare,
   "Valour and beauty! star on star!
"My eyes forbear the dazzling light,
"Of Halls so proud and visions bright."

The Minstrel struck his golden lyre,
   Boasting a world's renown,
The Knights looked up with eyes of fire,
   The Ladies soft looked down,

The King enchanted with the strain,
Bade them bring forth a golden chain.

" Nay load not me with chain of gold,
    " Such gifts become thy Knights,
" Noble by birth—in counsel bold,
    " First in a thousand fights.
" Or give it to thy Chancellor,—
" Who bears thy cares, the chain should wear.

" Free as the birds my notes I pour,
    " Who people wood and sward;
" The song that does spontaneous flow,
    " Is its own rich reward;
" Yet if one favour I may ask,
" Give me rich wine in golden flask."

The cup is brought, the wine is drank,
    " Oh sweet inspiring draught,
" All honor to the noble rank,
    " That counts such gift as naught,
" Grateful to Heav'n be thou, as I
" For this thy Lordly courtesy."

                                    GOETHE.

The German Baron.

"EST EST."

————⊷⊱⊰⊶————

Beside Bolsenor's yellow sands,
Where Flanschenberg its summit rears,
A solitary tombstone stands,
And this the epitaph it bears :—
      " Propter nimium est est
      " Dominus meus mortuus est."—
Beneath this monument, sleeps in grace
A Baron of ancient Teuton race ;
Capacious in courage, capacious in swallow,
God grant his sins may not him follow !
Over the Alps into Italie,
He rode with his Squire right cheerily,
But the wine was so thin, that at every cup,
He made a wry face, and his lips pursed up ;
So he said to his Squire " Go thou before,
" Every hostel and inn explore,

" Wherever the wines are oldest and best,

" There on the lintel write the word ' est.' "

So the Squire he rides and he rides before,

And he stops at every tavern door,

At every place, of every wine,

He tastes, and stops, if he deems it fine :

But where it is bad, he forbears to stay,

And in quest of better he rides away.

At length at that city himself he found,

For it's exquisite Muscatelle renowned,

No vintage in Italy rich or rare,

Could with that luscious wine compare :

The Squire as he drank it the beverage blest

And deemed it were wronged by a *single* " Est."

So in letters gigantic, with pencil red,

He painted " Est Est " on the doorway head.

The Baron he followed the signposts true,

And drank the best wine all the country through,

Till at last he 'lit on the Muscatelle,

Which his old Cup-bearer loved so well.

He came—he saw—he liked—he drank,

Till dead upon the ground he sank,

So the Squire and the Landlord, and waiters all,

Held a post mortem within the old Hall,

And a verdict found that 'twas fittest and best.

To bury him near to his loved Est Est.

On Flanschenbergs heights by Bolsenor fair.

So they dug him a grave and interred him there,

And over it raised a monument bare,

Without or name, or arms, or crest,

Save the short inscription before exprest :

Which means, in language of modern times,

As near as compatible with these rhymes—

" Here lies a man who drank himself dead,

" Of Muscatelle wine unprecedent-ed."

W. MÜLLER.

Die Waschfrau.

⸺

See you that aged woman there, beneath the linden tree,
Her years beyond our mortal span, toiling laboriously!
Long has she earned her bread with toil, and filled her duties sphere,
And borne the burthen of her lot, the lot assigned her here.
The fate of woman has been hers, sorrow and joy have done their part,
In youth she loved, and wore the ring, which binds the hand and heart.
Three pledges of her husband's love, three precious babes she bore.
His bed of sickness tended long, till death him from her tore ;
Then laid him in the grave, and placed, a stone above his head,
And thro' it all her faith endured, her patience never fled.
Her offspring were her earliest charge, to tend their budding youth,
To bring them up in loyalty, in honour and in truth;
The better for their wants to care, and for their means provide,
She tore her from her cherished home, and from her own fireside,
And there she stands alone, and old, without a tear or sigh,
But a courage born of faith, and a will to do, or die.

And well her fortitude has thriv'n, her prudence and her toil,
She's purchased flax, and worked it up, and burnt the midnight oil,
Her whirring wheel has spun the flax into the finest thread,
Wherewith the weaver linen weaves, for table and for bed,
And with the sempstress' skill and craft, she's fashioned neat and fair
The simple garb that in the grave, unconscious she will wear.
Her shroud she treasures in her chest, possession fond and dear,
It speaks a language of its own, reminding of her bier.
She wears it when with solemn step, she treads the sacred sod,
And wends her on the Sabbath morn, to offer prayers to God.
And I, oh, when my evening comes, my eventide of life,
And all its fitful joys are o'er, and all its petty strife,
When in the grave this form is laid, to crumble into dust,
May I be found as well prepared, as faithful to my trust,
And may I love my shroud and learn, the truths it tells as well
As yonder aged woman there, whose history I tell!

CHAMISSO.

The Maid and the Butterfly.

Over a meadow a maiden was straying,
In the ether above was a butterfly playing—
It lit on the fair maiden's lip.—
" How now," said the maid, " What impertinence this!"—
" I deemed 'twas a rosebud, and thought with a kiss
" From its petals sweet honey to sip."—
" This once I forgive thee," the maiden replied.
" But deem not my lips are a prey,
" For every butterfly on the hill side,
" That haps to be passing this way!"

CHAMISSO.

True unto Death.

Bound to the wars behold the noble Knight,
For freedom, fame, and native land to fight,
He pauses but his Lady love to see,
For well he deems a long farewell 'twill be—
  " Dim not with tears those eyes of blue,
    " Peace to thy heart should faith command,
  " For until death I'm leal and true,
    "To thee my love and Fatherland!"

His farewell said—he joins his faithful band,
And leaves his country for a foreign land,
Straight to the camp, and battle field he goes,
And looks undaunted on a host of foes.
  " I fear not war, I fear not death,
    " So thou prove true my trusty brand,
  " For I would give my latest breath,
    " For my true love, and fatherland !"

Behold him where the battle fiercest roars,
His soul like eagle o'er the carnage soars,
The field is theirs—and *his* the conquering band—
But see him lifeless stretched upon the sand—
    " Now flow my life blood, fleet my breath,
        I've venged me with my own right hand,
    I've kept my vow, true unto death,
        " To Lady love, and Fatherland ! "

THEODORE KÖRNER.

The Devil Outwitted.

The Devil once to the Hebrews came,
His breath was smoke and his lips were flame,
"One half of the world is mine," he cried,
"With you your harvest will I divide."

The Hebrews are wise, knowing good and ill,
So they offered the lower half to the Devil,
"No" said the fiend "my ambition soars,
"I will have the top of your crops and stores."

So the Hebrews sowed turnips in the ground,
And when the time of harvest came round,
The Hebrews they took the rich root crops,
While the Devil put up with the turnip tops.

But when next season again he came,
The Devil he spoke with rage and scorn,
"The lower half this time I claim,"
So the Hebrews they planted wheat and corn.

But when again the division came,
The ears of the corn to the Hebrews fell,
So the Devil was left the straw to claim,
And with that he heats the ovens of Hell!

REICHART.

The Faithful Comrade.

———⋙⋅⋘———

I once had a Comrade faithful and true,
Wherever I went he was sure to go too,
He would never go out if I loitered at home,
But whene'er I went forth he was certain to come,
We slept in one bed, and drank from one glass,
He went with me even to visit my lass.
One day with my knapsack and staff I set out,
But I could not leave home my companion without.
As we quitted the City, the Zephyrs blew sweet,
And the trees and the gardens our senses did greet ;
But my friend he looked grave, and shook sadly his head,
As if with the vision disquiet-ed.
A chorus of larks in the ether we hear,
But my Comrade he frowns and stops closely his ear,
The sweetest of perfumes are borne on the gale,
But my friend he grows faint and his visage is pale ;

Then higher and higher I climbed the steep hill,
But he loitered behind, as if weary and ill.
I stood by myself on the summit so high,
The sun it was bright in the vapourless sky,
On the glorious mountain's precipitate top
It was needs for a moment that I should stop
But alas coming down I unwarily tread
On the lifeless corpse of my comrade dead.
I dug him a grave and I buried him there,
And his tomb did this sad inscription bear :—

Here lies Sir Hypocondriasis,

His life was a burden—his end was bliss,

Of songs, and flowers and fresh air he died.

And a thousand (to him) like ills beside,

I wish him joy and felicity,

For ever and ever wherever he be,

But much as I dwell on his memory here,

May he never, in life, to me re-appear !

ANASTASIUS GRÜN.

The Flower's Revenge.

Upon a couch a maid lies hushed,
    At hour of midnight rest;
Her cheeks with crimson glow are flushed,
    Her eyes with sleep opprest.

On a table near her set,
    Stands a vase of flowers,
Bright as gems—fresh gathered, wet
    With summer's dewy showers.

The chamber glows with stifling heat,
    The casement's closed with care;
The room distils with fragrance sweet,
    No breath disturbs the air.

Around night's stillness reigns profound,
    A silence as of death,
When from the flowers a whispering sound,
    Comes like the Zephyr's breath.

O

And now from every blossom seems,
    A vap'ry mist to exhale,
And shadowy forms as seen in dreams,
    Clad in mysterious veil.

From out the bosom of the rose,
    A lady bright appears,
Her hair, like golden streamlet flows,
    Studded with pearly tears.

From out the monk's hood's purple crest,
    Set in its emerald leaves,
A knight steps forth with steel-clad breast,
    And helmet, sword, and greaves.

Upon his crest the heron's grey plume,
    Floats o'er his shoulders mailed,
While from the lily's virgin bloom,
    Appears a maiden veiled.

From out the turk's caps yellow lining,
    A negro dark is seen,
A golden crescent brightly shining,
    Upon his turban green.

From the sweet narcissus flowers,
    Whence the bee its honey sips,
Steps a youth, and eager show'rs
    Kisses on the maiden's lips.

Dancing then in circle round,
  The spirits skip and sing,
And the maiden sleeps profound,
  While their airy voices sing—

"Maiden! maiden! from the earth,
  " Thou hast torn us ruthlessly,
" Borne us from our place of birth,
  " Here to fade and die!

" In the lap of mother earth,
  " Happy was our lot, and gay!
" Gladsome, joyous, full of mirth,
  " Basking in the sun's warm ray.

" Cooled by breezes soft of spring
  " Playing with our slender stems,
" Elf-like danced we in a ring,
  " When the stars shone bright as gems.

" Rain and dew refreshed us then,
  " Here we languish, pine, and die!
" Thou who placed us in this den,
  " Know that our revenge is nigh."—

The song is hushed, the spirits bow
  The maiden's couch around,
And in the solemn stillness now,
  Is heard the whispering sound.

The spirits breathe, the spirits blow,
  The flowers exhale a faint perfume ;
The maiden's cheeks more brightly glow,
  A stifling odour fills the room.

And now the morning sun peeps in,
  The spirits all have fled ;
And there, with visage pale and thin,
  The lovely maid lies dead.

A blossom nipt in early bloom,
  Her sister flowers beside,
Their loved perfume has been her doom,
  Cut off in beauty's pride.

FREILIGRATH.

The Wanderer's Song.

The wine has been drunk,
    Of our parting the token,
Adieu to our gathering,
    The word must be spoken.

Farewell to these hills,
    And the home of my youth ;
I must leave you, tho' dearly
    I love you in truth.

My soul is athirst,
    Dear friends of my heart,
Its fetters to burst,
    Now at last we must part.

The sun in the heavens,
    It never is still,
It moves o'er the waters,
    The valley, the hill.

The breath of the tempest,
    The waves of the ocean,
They rest themselves never,
    But are always in motion.

The clouds do but follow,
    The migrating swallow,
And man in his wand'rings
    Thro' every nation,
Conforms to the laws
    Of the whole of creation.

The birds as they pass him,
    Are fresh from his home,
The perfumes that charm him,
    From his own garden come,

He knew them in youth,
    In his own Fatherland,
He planted and tended
    With fond lover's hand.

They greet him abroad,
    As companions and friends,
And make him a bright home,
    Wherever he wends.

                  KERNER.

The Child of Care.

" Care " sat beside a murmuring stream,
 Her thoughts absorbed as in a dream,
And with her fingers modelled there,
 In plastic clay, a statue fair.

" Goddess of thought, what dost thou, say ? "
 Spoke Jove descending from above,—
" I mould a human form in clay,—
 " Oh! give it life, almighty Jove."—

" So be it !—let it live !—it lives !—
 " But mine must the creation be,
" For mine the power its being gives."—
 " Nay Jove, the man belongs to me.

" My hand it was that fashioned it."—
 " But I " said Jove " that gave it life."—
While thus they spoke Earth's God alit,
 And complicated thus the strife—

"Ye powers, the man is mine by birth,
  " He took his substance from the Earth."
" Well, well " said Jove " we'll waive debate,
  " Here's Saturn—he shall arbitrate."

Then Saturn speaks—" The Immortals will,
  " This being born to good and ill,
" To Jove—to Earth—and Care, to thee,
  A common heritage shall be.

" To Jove, who gave, his soul belongs,
  " To Earth, his native clay must go.
" Nor thee, oh Care, my judgment wrongs,
  " He shall be thine his lifetime through.

" Thou Care, thy child wilt ne'er forsake,—
  " While here he draws his mortal breath,
" With doubt and fear his heart will ache,
  " Till thou resign'st him loth to death."

Thus Saturn spoke the eternal doom,—
  Care is man's guardian from the tomb,
His bones to kindred Earth are given,
  His soul returns to God in heav'n.

      HERDER.

The Beggar and his Dog.

What ! for my Dog, five shillings pay ?
    You almost take away my breath,
What means this new extortion—say ?
    This persecution unto death ?

I am a poor sick man—so old,
    That not a penny can I earn,
I have no bread, I have no gold,
    Hunger and grief where'er I turn.

When grew I sick, when I grew old,
    Who had compassion on my lot ?
Who warmed me when my limbs were cold ?
    Or visited my humble cot ?

P

Who sheltered when the chill wind blew?
    Who soothed me when I groaned with pain?
Who shared my hunger, fond and true,
    Content to starve, yet ne'er complain?

My dog, my life and yours decline,
    What fate awaits us? yours is mine,
We both alike are old and sick,
    The hand would drown thee thou dost lick

Is this thy guerdon? this thy end?—
    The common lot, my humble friend!
Ah! well, I've been in many a fight,
    But ne'er a murderer till to night.—

There lies the rope, the stone is there,
    The pool is near, so now prepare,—
Come—but oh! look not thus on me,
    T'is but a plunge—'tis o'er with thee.

O'er the dog's head the noose he threw,
    He wagged his tail, and licked his face.
The man recoiled—the noose withdrew—
    And o'er his own head did it place.

A fearful oath he muttered then,
    He cursed both Gods and fellow-men,
Then plunged into the depths below—
    The opening waters o'er him flow.

His faithful dog who saw him sink,
　　Howled to the boatman from the shore,
Then plunging dragged him to the brink—
　　Alas! the old man is no more!

So they carried him thence, thro' midnight's gloom,
　　His Dog, sole mourner to the tomb,
And where o'er his grave the earth did close,
　　The Dog lay down and never rose.

　　　　　　　　　　CHAMISSO.

The Blind Widow.

Who enters the doorway so quietly, anxiously?
  'Tis the Widow's—the deaf Widow's son,
She sits at her wheel, so silently, wearily,—
  She heard not his step as she spun.

He sprang to her side, so joyously lovingly,—
  "Oh, Mother! dear Mother!" he breathed in low tone,—
The sight of her lost one long sought so despairingly,
  Worked a charm on the widow so lone.

Her deaf ears were opened, the premature traces
  Of sorrow and age like a vision depart,
As she clasped him so close in a mother's embraces,
  She heard the quick beat of his heart.

And now as she sits in the glorious sunbeams,
  The light in her breast is as cheering and bright,
Her Spirit is soaring once more in her day dreams,
  And she hears the sweet songs of the angels of light.

CHAMISSO.

The Fisherman.

A Fisherman sat by the river side,
    Listlessly, musingly ;
His heart was still, as the rod by his side,
    While the bubbling stream rolled silently.

There as he sat him, in mute repose,
    A wave stood up in air,
And out of the parted waters rose,
    A maiden with dripping hair.

" Mortal," she sang, with her voice so sweet,
    " Why practice thine art to snare
" The finny tribe from their calm retreat,
    " Down in the hollows there ?

" Didst thou but know how joyously,
    " They sport them there below,
" Gladly thou'dst come and dwell with me,
    " Where the waters softly flow.

" The Sun and Moon in Ocean lave

   " Their glorious orbs at night,

" And mirrored in this shimmering wave,

   " Thy brow seems doubly bright.

" See'st thou, transparent in the stream,

   " Heaven's vault of azure blue,

" See'st in its light thy features seem,

   " Steeped in ambrosial dew ? "

     The waters rose,

     The waters rose,

  They washed the Fisher's feet ;—

     The maiden sung,

     The maiden sung,

  With voice so low and sweet,—

  The Fisher seemed as in a dream ;

     Then down the bank,

     He slipped and sank,

  For ever in the stream !

GOETHE.

Spring.

The Season has doffed its rough wintery robe
Of darkness and mist that enveloped the globe.
    And has donned its soft mantle of lace ;
Bright sunshine illumines the earth and the sky,
And Creation enraptured unites in the cry
    Of praise to the Lord for the mercy and grace,
Which has torn from the earth its rough wintery robe
Of darkness and mist that enshrouded the globe.

CHARLES MARTEL.

The Emperor and the Abbot.

A Monarch once lived, and a good Monarch, too,—
　　An Abbot, a jolly old monk of his cloth,
And his Shepherd, the cleverer man of the two,
　　In wit and in cunning a match for them both.

The Emperor oft in his steel harness slept,
　　And suffered from hunger, from heat, and from cold,
While the Abbot looked pursy, and sleek and well kept,
　　And in gait like a ponderous beer barrel rolled.

The Monarch was riled at the burly Priest's mien,
　　And one day as he rode in the sun's burning rays,
At the head of his squadron, he vented his spleen
　　On the Abbot's fat form, and luxurious ways.

He greeted him rudely, with jeer, and with jest,
" Thou servant of Heaven, most faithful and blest,
" How fare ye ? 'Twould seem by thy looks that with thee
" Long fastings and prayers and devotions agree.

" Yet, saving your Reverence, seems it to me,
" You must suffer from vapours at times, and *ennui*,
" They say you're the cleverest man in the land,
" Can hear the grass grow, and can number the sand.

" So now I will give you some work for your head,
    " Some nuts for your jolly sharp grinders to crack ;
" Two months will I give you my riddle to read,
    " You must answer by then, or I give you the sack.

" And first I must ask you, my Treasurer great,
" When I sit on my throne in my Council of State,
" (And let not the question your reason o'erwhelm)
" You must tell me my value in coin of the realm.

" And next I must ask you—How long would it need
" To circle the globe on my gallant war steed ?
" You must tell me precisely the time to a day,
" To you such a question is merely child's play.

" And thirdly, most noble of prelates, I swear,
" The thoughts of my mind you must fully declare,
" To the letter I bid you reveal them in sooth,
" Tho' there be not in one, a scintilla of truth.

" And an ye shall fail to respond to my call,
" Sir Abbot, no longer you're Priest of St. Galle ;
" You shall ride on a donkey throughout the whole land,
" Your face to his rump, and his tail in your hand."

Q

Then laughing the Emperor went on his way,
The Abbot stood motionless, blank with dismay,
No criminal ever the scaffold drew nigh,
With pangs of more terrible agony.

He sought Universities, two, three, and four,
He consulted the faculties over and o'er,
He encountered expenses and paid honoraires,
But in vain, they all left him in hopeless despair.

In his trouble and anguish, hours grew into days,
And days into weeks, of misdoubt and malaise,
And as it drew nearer, the hour of his doom,
The light in his eyes turned to darkness and gloom.

With attenuate form—with cheeks sunken and pale,
He wandered alone over hill and by dale,
Till one day, on a track with huge boulders beset,
Hans Bendricks his shepherd he suddenly met.

Quoth Bendricks " Sir Abbot, what ails you I pray ?
" To a ghost you are shrunken, and fallen away,
" And your breathing is short, and you cough on my word,
" Some trouble disturbs you, 'tis plain, my good Lord."

"Alas! my good Bendricks, alas! 'tis too true,
" The Emp'ror has given me a task I must do,
"A nut which the Devil himself could not crack,
" Tho' assisted by hell's every imp at his back.

" He bids me to tell him his value in coin,
" When in Council his Lords and his Councillors join,
" He exacts I should tell him how long it would need,
" To circle the globe on his gallant war steed ;

" The thoughts of his heart, to discover them all,
" Or to cease to continue the Priest of St. Galle,
" And be dragged on an ass thro' the breadth of the land,
" With my face to his rump, and his tail in my hand."

" Is that all ?—now take courage—Sir Priest of St. Galle,
" Such questions as these I can answer them all,
" Only lend me thy crozier and robes—and alone
" I will kneel, in thy stead, at the Emperor's throne.

" 'Tis true that of Latin I know scarce a word,
" Yet I know how a snare to avoid, like a bird,
" And riches are pow'rless such learning to buy,
" As Dame Nature's best gift, mother wit, will supply."

The Abbot he skipped like a goat with delight,
And quickly Hans Bendricks with mantle was dight,
And crozier and cowl and canonicals all,
And despatched to the court as the Priest of St. Galle.

There high on his throne in Imperial state,
With crown and with sceptre the Emperor sate—
" Now tell me, my Treasurer great I enjoin,
" Now, tell me, precisely, my value in coin."

" My Liege," said the Abbot, " Our Saviour of old,
" For thirty pieces of silver was sold,
" It will not be treason, your Grace will confess,
" To rate you (great king tho' you be) at one less."

The Monarch looked puzzled—but at length he replied,
" By my faith ! you have reason, fat Monk, on your side,
" Though in sooth, on my honor, Sir Priest, I admit,
" I was not prepared to encounter such wit.

" But now you're to tell me how long it will need
" To circle the world on my gallant war steed ;
" Not one minute too little, or much, must you say,
" Is this riddle as easy, fat Abbot, I pray ? "

" Sir King," said the Priest, " if you mount with the sun,
" And with him his day's course, thro' the heavens will run,
" Two days will behold you encircle the earth,
" And belt its circumference as with a girth."

" Ha ! ha ! shrewdly guessed," said the King with a smile,
" With your ' ifs ' and your ' buts,' and your cunning and guile,
" Sir Priest, you're a right clever fellow I own,
" I would back you to find the philosopher's stone.

" But now for my third (you will answer with ease),
" But none of your ' ifs ' and your ' buts,' if you please,—
" Now tell me the thoughts in my bosom that stir,
" And prove they are false, or the forfeit incur."

" My Liege, that is easy—you're thinking that I
" Am the Priest of St. Galle."—"That I do not deny."
" But you're wholly mistaken—I'm nothing at all,
" But the shepherd and serf of the monks of St. Galle!"

" The devil! you are not the Priest of St. Galle!"
The Emperor cried, and seemed ready to fall ;—
Then smiling, he added, "but if thou'rt not he,
" My friend, rest assured, very soon thou shalt be ;"

" With the mitre and crozier I thee will invest,
" The Abbot shall ride on a donkey full drest ;
" But I warn thee, my friend, holy lore must thou read,—
" Who would harvest the grain, must first scatter the seed.

" With your favor, great Emp'ror, that never will do,
" Both reading and writing and sums I eschew,
" Of Latin I know but a sentence or so,
" And what little Jack learnt not, John never can know."

" Nay, that is unlucky, good Bendricks, but still,
" Pray ask me a favor, whatever you will :
" You have pleased me so much with your shrewdness and wit,
" I would gladly repay you, if you will permit."

" Great Monarch, I would not be rich or be great,
" A boon would you grant me ; now, deign reinstate,
" Once more in your favor, the Priest of St. Galle,
" I should reckon such kindness the greatest of all."

" Now, bravo ! good fellow, your word I believe,

" And your heart is as good as your head, I perceive ;

" So be it—the Abbot his place shall retain,

" And you, for reward, plain Hans Bendricks remain.

" But no more must you tend the lean sheep of St. Galle,

" With an order of merit I will thee instal,

" The Abbot shall tend thee, a time-honored guest,

" Till in fulness of years thou inherit thy rest ! "

BÜRGER.

Nero.

Grey in the purple firmament of Heaven,
Rise the gigantic buildings of old Rome,
On Tiber's stream a gondola is borne,
Gently adown the current's rippling wave,
Cushioned on curtains rich, and soft as down,
A slight fair youth with flowing locks reclines,
His heart now wildly beats, and now is still,—
'Tis Nero! Not the Imperial crown he wears,
Which clasps too tightly his voluptuous brow ;
A wreath of roses, with celestial hue,
Crowns the rich splendor of his golden locks.
His eyes are fixed on Rome's far-spreading walls,—
What seeks he there, with such impatient gaze ?
He groans—he sighs—his bosom heaves and falls,—
" What means this silence, will it ne'er begin ?"—
And now a tongue of lambent flame shoots forth,
And lights the darkness of the deep blue sky,

Now far and wide the angry flames burst out,
And coil like serpents from a thousand roofs.
With blood-red light the heavens are overspread,
And Tiber's waves reflect the crimson glow,—
Above, below, a double arch of flame
Glows like a furnace in the sky and stream ;
Midway the bark with measured stroke glides on.
The golden cups resplendent in the light,
The rich wine sparkling with a ruddier hue,
And Nero—clothed with arbitrary power,
He acts the God, as if the world were his
To make and to destroy ; and his blood boils
With dreams of self-assumed omnipotence.
Gorged to satiety with human blood,
Strife of wild beasts, and immolated slaves,
He covets horror on a mightier scale
To feed his pampered appetite for woe.
The world's great autocrat, in wanton power,
His wild distraught imagination fired,
To light again the embers of his lust,
With new excitement and emotion burns,
While Rome consumes in suicidal flame.
See now the light plays softly o'er his brows,
The wreath of flowers is red with crimson fire,
It plays refulgent in his flashing eyes,
And paints the rose upon his finger tips,

That tremble on the lute's vibrating strings,
Till roused to fire, he strikes the grandest chords,
And sings the dirge of Homer's tragic song,
How Ilium fought and perished in the flame.
Oft has he sung the ruin of the world ;
Never till now he realised the tale
When Rome lies there, enveloped in the fire.
How life-like now the soft Greek lines proclaim
The dying splendor of the burning world !
How now, his mind embraces all the truth
Of the immortal bard's heroic strains ;
He hears the anguish of unnumbered cries,—
The wail of victims, till his wild tears flow,
And steeped in deep emotion he sinks down,
The prey alike of nature and of art.
Now is the half of Rome in ashes laid,
Fades the last glow and dies the latest wail.
The thrilling chords are lost upon the breeze,
And with them pass a thousand fleeting lives.
Empress of Earth ! and is it come to this,
That thou, the mightiest city of the world
Must perish ! that thy Emperor may feel
The stirring beauties of a poet's lay !
And is it so ? that thy Imperial Lord,
Decked as a woman, and with lute and song,
Declaimer—actor—dancer—all in one,

R

Holds in his hand the destinies of earth !
'Tis so—The morrow, in well acted rage,
He brands the Nazarenes with all his crimes,
" Seize them and slay ! " he cries, as if in wrath,
But only that, in scenes of deadlier guilt
His soul may drink more deep of tragic woe !
But now, inhuman monster ! know that thou
Hast struck the knell of thine eternal doom ;
Thy sceptre trembles in thy palsied hand,
There lives not one, that asked, will give thee death,
Yet thou shalt meet a miserable doom !
The slaughtered Nazarenes now bear the Cross ;
But see, the day approaches when that Cross,
Symbol of everlasting rule on earth,
Shall triumph o'er the Imperial Diadem !

SALLES.

The Wandering Jew.

From out the deepest cave in Carmel's side
Issued the Wandering Jew of God accurst.
Two thousand weary years well nigh had past,
Since seeking rest, in every land and clime
His spell bound feet had wandered, from the time
When Jesus sinking 'neath the cruel Cross,
Essayed to rest before Ahastos' door ;
But he, unknowing pity, did refuse
Short respite to the Saviour's worn-out frame,
And drove with scorn the victim from his door.—
The Man of Sorrows tottered and sank down,
But murmur uttered none.   Then stepped there forth
The Angel of God's wrath, and thus addrest
The wretched man : " Monster of earth !
" Who from thy door the Son of Man hast spurned,
" To thee for ever be repose denied.
" A demon dark of hell shall dog thy steps
" From shore to shore,—to thee the wretch's friend,
" Death and the grave shall refuge offer none."—

Now from the cavern dark Ahastos strode,

And shook his grizzly beard, and seized a skull

From off the piled up heap, and hurled it down ;

Crashing, it rolled, and shivered 'gainst a rock.

" That was my father's skull," Ahastos howled,

" And these, and these," with glaring eyes, he raved,

As down he hurled seven bleached and hollow skulls,

That leaped from rock to rock, " These were my wives !

" And these " (as poured the torrent) " were my children.

" All they *could* die, *have* died ; but I accurst

" Am doomed to live this living death for ever—

" Wretch that I am ! When fell Jerusalem,

" I courted death, I slew the innocents,

" I rushed into the flames, I cursed the Roman.—

" But it was vain, the deep eternal curse

" Bound me to life—I must not, could not, die !

" Time ran its course ; and Rome in ruins lay.

" I crept beneath its crumbling structures, but in vain ;

" They fell, but falling, would not give me death;

" Kingdoms grew up around me, and they fell,

" Their fall I witnessed, but I shared it not ;

" I cast me from the mountains, capped with clouds,

" Into the depths below of boiling waves,

" But all in vain, the waters cast me up,

" And on the desert shore I woke to feel

" The piercing arrows of my doomed existence.

" Downward I gazed on Etna's dark abyss,

" Then madly plunged into its burning floods,

" Ten months I lived in agony within

" Its seething cauldron ; ten long weary months

" I filled its sulphurous crater with my groans ;

" But Etna boiled and vomited me forth,

" In streams of lava, stifled, yet alive.

" I saw a blazing forest—mad I rushed

" Into the burning furnace—from the trees

" The fire-flakes fell, and singed my grizzly hair,

" They scorched my bones, but still consumed me not.

" For me the tiger's pointed fangs were dull,

" The lion in the arena tore me not.

" The arm of executioner was palsied,—

" I made my bed with serpents, but the asp

" And deadliest of vipers, tho' they stung,

" Forebore to take my miserable life.

" I seized the dragon by his blood-red crest,

" He bit and tortured, but refused me death.

" I braved the world's great tyrants, and defied,

" Denounced the monster Nero to his face,

" I cursed, as renegades, the Christian race,

" And Mulei Ismael as a bloodhound styled.

" For me new tortures and new forms of death

" The tyrants compassed, but destroyed me not,·—

" Unhappy wretch, I must not, could not die !

" For me no rest, nor respite in the grave !

" Doomed to eternity to bear the garb

" Of mortal clay, and dust, reeking of death,

" And pestilence, and the dark charnel vault,

" Here must I face eternity, and time

" For centuries successive,—time that begets

" Her children and consumes them.   But for me

" No rest on earth, no refuge in the grave !

" Oh ! dread Avenger in the heavens above,

" Say, hast thou not in thy dark arsenal

" Some doom still darker, punishment more fell ?

" Then hurl thy bolt upon my devoted head.

" Would that the tempest of thy wrath might burst,

" And cast me from the height of Carmel's mount,

" And that outstretched and gasping I might lie,

" Prone at its base and breathe my latest sigh."

Ahastos sank—a sound was in his ear,

Night gently closed his weary eyelids there :

An Angel bore him to the cave again,

And said, " Ahastos ! thou may'st rest at last,

" Sleep a sweet sleep—God's wrath at length is past."

SHUBART.

Blucher.

From wing to wing, along the British lines
Stretched there a pathway—and beside the road
Which intersected the right flank, there stood
Upon the green hill-side, a tree, and there
Beneath its shade stood Wellington—
Anxious—with watch in hand, care on his brow,
He weighed his fortunes, with his tale of dead—
" Hours must elapse, and still our ranks be thinned,
" Ere Blucher's force can reach the battle field."
" I come " cried Blucher, loyal to his word,
And leal in spirit to his brother chief ;
" I come, I come," a thousand times he cried.
And while he spoke, from off his rugged brow
The streams poured down, sign of his body's toil,
And of his soul's impatience—to the spot
Bound as by spells, his struggling arms were chained.
Nature with all her elemental powers
Lashed into wrath, opposed her storm-born son.
The clouds gush forth, the streams o'erflowing rise,
Pools become lakes, dams burst, and bridges fall.

The clay is liquid—and a slimy marsh
Sucks in, and holds resistless, man and horse,
And all the vast materiel of war.—
Hills rise before them, on their labored way,
And in their sandy arms enclose—the wheels
Sink in, the axles break, and man and beast
Lie struggling, cursing, whip and goad applied
In vain—the Prussian force in broken ranks
Stands fixed—imbedded and immoveable.
No power of man, no brutal force of beast
Can war with heaven. I hear the thunder roar,
The lightnings flash—the march thro' Wavre becomes
The path of hell. " Forwards! who hell confronts
" Must tread its paths and thro' its mazes pass."
And thro' they go. Wavre lies in mist behind.—
" What force is that behind us ? " " Grouchy, Prince,
" With more than 30,000 bayonets ;
" He presses on us—we must battle give."—
" Not so, before lies Waterloo, and we
" Are thither bound," replies the grey-haired chief,
Who sees his Cæsar's Ides of March draw near.
" Forward ! your ranks close up. But what is this ?
" The wood is full, and we must fight our way !"—
Hark, from the gates a voice ! " Courage ! " it cries,
" The roads are free, the wood unoccupied,
" As true as I am Grollmann !"—Can it be ?—

" No Prussians there? and yet the wood is free!

" This is the act, of Buonaparte—or *God*.

" Forward ! in God's name forward ! " Blucher cries—

In vain they toil—they struggle, but in vain.

Firm as a rock, yet motionless, the troops

Essay to form—'tis vain—from out the mud—

From out the hollow causeways comes the cry

" 'Tis vain."—Meantime above the storm and din

Thunders the British battle. Blucher hears,

In spirit sees the battle field, and hears

The groans of agony—the cries for help,

He knows his Brother Chief opposed at last

In mortal strife to Europe's haughty foe

Upon a field, where dubious hangs the fate

Of the world's continent. His heavy heart

Is weighted with his promise. Aides announce

The Emp'ror's last great charge—the need of help,

And Blucher storm-bound, sees his eager troops

Chained to the spot, tho' all the roads are free !

" Children," he cries, " well may you say 'tis vain

" With human force to combat Nature's laws,

" Yet to my brother Chief my word is gaged,

" You would not have it broken, I your Father

" Bid you to help me keep it,"

And 'twas kept.

SCHERENBERG.

S

Belshazzar.

—·°:♥:°—

'Twas midnight's hour well nigh, and all was still
Within the walls of Babylon the Great,
Save where Belshazzar in his halls of state
Brilliant with gold, and gems—held revel high.
Around his Courtiers and his vassals ranged
Quaffed the red flowing juice in cups of gold
And mirth waxed riotous as wine prevailed.
The King looked on with ever glowing cheek,
The fumes of wine his impious courage fired.
He cursed the Lord with sacrilegious breath,
While thousand voices bellowed forth applause.
With glance of pride, the monarch called a slave,
The slave retires—then hastily returns—
Upon his head he bears the vessels all of gold,
In God's high temple, dedicate to Heav'n—
With hand presumptuous the Monarch grasps
A golden cup, and fills it to the brim,
Then drains the liquid to the lowest drop,

And shouts in accents impiously bold
" Jehovah, God of Heav'n, I thee defy—
" I, only I, am King of Babylon ! "
He said, but, scarcely had the words gone forth,
A dread unutterable seized his heart,
The mirth that late had sounded thro' the hall
Was hushed—deep silence reigned throughout the crowd ;
And there! and there! upon the marble wall
Appeared the semblance of a mighty hand.
It wrote—it wrote—upon the marble wall
Letters of fire—it wrote—and disappeared.
The Monarch sat—with horror on his brow,
With trembling limbs, and eyeballs fixed and glazed.
A chill of terror thrilled in every breast,
A death-like stillness ruled the multitude.
Magicians came, their art they tried in vain,
Not one could read the writing on the wall.
But ere the morning dawned Belshazzar lay
A bleeding corpse within his palace walls.

HEINE.

The Opal Ring.

―∘:∘:∘―

Far in the east, there dwelt in times bygone
A man to fame and public life unknown ;
The Patriarch of his tribe, a gentle race,
Whose sons were brave, whose daughters fair of face.
A friend he had, who shared his hearth and heart,
Skilled in the lore of necromantic art,
Ancient of years, in manner cold and stern,
His heart could yet with warm affection burn,
He loved the sire, he loved the noble race,
The sons so brave, the daughters fair of face.
And oft he talked and mused, of what would be
When he was gone, their future destiny.
No wealth they had, and he had none to leave,
And therefore he would often sigh and grieve.
One eve, the friends sate by the ocean wave
And talked and thought of things beyond the grave ;
The moon rose full from out the ocean blue,
Tinged with the parting sunbeams roseate hue,
Night had assumed, on earth, her sable robe,
But noon reigned glorious in that crimson globe.

The stars above in glittering radiancy,
Cast streams of light across the purple sea.
Calm as a lake, and silent as the grave,
No sound disturbed, no ripple broke the wave.
It was a scene from which the human mind
Soars upward, leaving earthly things behind,
And the soul sighs for light to penetrate
The hidden mysteries of a future state—
Thus, when they long had sat, the old man broke
The silence, and in mournful accents spoke—
" Friend of my youth, my time is ebbing fast,
" The dream of life, to me, is well nigh past.
" I go, I know not where, but as the night
" Around us, wants not gleams of brilliant light,
" So in my heart a spark of heav'n-born hope
" Radiates the darkness of my horoscope.
" I leave thee still a traveller on the road,
" Which leads us all at last to one abode,
" Yet ere we part, accept this opal ring,
" Hope's flickering type, a friendship's offering,
" Nor deem it worthy for the gem alone—
" It boasts a worth inherent of its own.
" A charm it owns, who wears it, where he goes
" Is loved and feared alike by friends and foes.
" Foremost in camp and hall, by land and sea,
" He shines with all the opal's brilliancy,

" Nor less in wisdom does his mind excel,
" And truth and virtue in his bosom dwell."
The old man died, the ring descending passed
From sire to son, an heirloom, till at last
It came to one, a chief, supremely blest
With two brave sons, the noblest and the best
Of all the tribes around—so had the mystic stone
Worked wonders in the generations gone.
The sire was wise, affectionate, and true,
The powers of that miraculous gem he knew ;
He loved his sons with all a father's love,
Not one below the other, one above,
He heard the step of death behind him tread,
He felt the cold hand on his shoulder laid,
His treasured gift, his heritage from heaven,
To which of his two sons should it be given ?
By day he thought, by night he dreamed, but still
Decision came not to his wavering will :
He could not choose between his sons to bless,
The one more richly and the other less.
At length an erring judgment, born of love,
But not discriminating, did him move
To an expedient—he enlisted Art,
Of the fair ring to work a counterpart.
So well the artist wrought, that no one knew
(As oft in this life happens) false from true,

The dying man each son in secret blest
And gave to each the ring, or so professed—
The old man passed—the secret soon was known
Each brother claimed the heirloom for his own,
Each deemed the others ring a counterfeit,
And soon an angry flame of wrath was lit,
The brothers' love to furious hate was turned,
And rage and envy in each bosom burned.
They sought the Cadi, each his story told,
The Judge with patient bearing listened cold.
"Whence the dispute? each has an opal ring
"A father's gift—affection's offering—
"'Tis said a mystic power of good unknown
"Dwells in the lustre of the precious stone,
"But which ye know not—why not equal both—
"Say if ye can—and I will hear your oath—
"Ye venture not! neither can truly say
"The blessing dwells but in his opal's ray?
"What if the ring be lost—its virtue gone—
"Your Sire misgave the working of the stone,
"And willed his sons in life should equal be
"In lot alike—in choice and action free—
"Let time decide—each brother keep his own,
"Doubt not the merits of the radiant stone,
"Expel the fiend of envy from each breast,
"Trust in your father's blessing and be blest!"

LESSING.

The Friar of Orders Grey.

' Sir Knight," the lady said, and a tear was in her eye,
And her voice was low and mournful, as the breathing of a sigh :
  " Sir Knight, I would it were so, or that ever it could be,
" From childhood, I have known thee, as a friend I love thee dearly,
" For thy valour and thy prowess I honour and revere thee,
  " But the love that thou desirest, I cannot give to thee."

The Knight he bowed him lowly, as the cruel words were spoken,
When he left that lady's presence, his heart was well nigh broken,
  But the soul within him triumphed over words so hard and cold,
He summoned his retainers, and armed with bow and blade,
To join the Sacred warfare, the Christian cavalcade,
  And wrest the Holy Sepulchre from Unbelievers' hold.

And soon his fame was known, throughout the Paynim land,
Where'er the fray was thickest, his courser trod the sand,
  His blade was reddest dyed, his lance drank noblest gore,
His band of heroes glutted them, like lions in the fold,
His banner waved conspicuous, with crimson and with gold,
  But the leader's heart was far away on Europe's distant shore.

A year and more had passed, a year of pain and grief,
Nor time, nor war's distraction brought solace or relief
    For sorrow of his lady love, to that unhappy Knight—
He pined to breathe the air she breathed, to sun him in her smile—
In Joppa's port, a friendly bark lay bound for Britain's isle—
    He joined the ship, and sick at heart, withdrew him from the fight.

Many a weary night and day they ploughed the boiling seas,
He revelled in the stormy blast, and wooed the softer breeze,
    For they bore him where he last had left that maiden wan and pale—
He reached at length the castle gate—"What would ye here, Sir Knight?
" My Lady treads these halls no more—It was but yesternight
    " In yonder cloister, in the isle, she took the convent veil."

From that day forth his Father's halls no more their Master knew.
No more in field his banner waved, in camp his bugle blew,
    His noble steed in freedom ranged the forest's grassy waste—
That night unchallenged thro' the gate a stranger took his way
In garb and mien and gait he seemed a Friar of Orders Grey,
    His cassock was of camel's hair, and a cord was round his waist.

And on a rock above the spot where the Convent peaceful slept,
And lindens whispered to the breeze and bending willows wept,
    A hut of unhewn stone appeared, with entrance rude and low,
And by it sate, from morn till eve, a Friar of Orders Grey.
Lonely he sate—and gazed and wept, lonely the livelong day,
    His face was sad—but hope seemed there, like a sunbeam on his brow.

T

And there for many a weary month, and many a weary year,
The hermit kept his anxious guard over the convent near,
    He watched the casement opposite, and oftentimes he wept,
But when at eve it opened wide, and in the vacant frame
A face as pure and peaceful as the blest Madonna came,
    His weary task seemed recompensed and he laid him down and slept.

Years wore away, and still the sun looked down from morn to eve,
Upon the Friar of Orders Grey whose grief knew no reprieve,
    And still he watched the casement dear, till came the angel face—
One morn they found him seated there, still on his lonely watch,
Until his eye should greet that form, that lovely vision catch,
    But the gazing orbs were visionless, and a corpse was in his place.

SCHMIDT VON LUBECH.

The History of the Hat.

When hats there were none, but of iron or brass,
    And the only mails known were of plate or of chain,
And beavers were steel, that the lance might not pass
    Thro' the bars to the eye and the brain,

An original mortal invented a hat
    Like a pot without shape, without band, without brim,
'Twas waterproof too, with the skin of a cat,
    It's fault, was, if any, it's wearer looked grim.

His neighbours applauded the novel essay,
    Was there ever a mortal so fertile of brain ?
The design was astounding, the taste recherchée,
    No wonder the man was elated and vain.

But one day he died—as the wisest will do,
    And he left his chef d'œuvre (as needs must) to his heir,
Who devoted his thoughts to invent something new,
    With the worthy ambition to make people stare.

The result of his deep lucubrations was this:
　　To his forefather's hat he adapted a brim,
And his neighbours applauded and praised him, I wis
　　Till the shade of his father's great mem'ry grew dim.

But he died; and the improvised hat of his sire,
　　With it's novel adornment descended again,
And the heir with his forefather's genius on fire
　　Decreed its appearance decidedly plain.

So he decked it with ribbons before and behind,
　　And strutted like peacock, elate, on his way,
Till his neighbours pronounced him the pride of mankind,
　　The genius, the marvel, the soul of his day.

But he also died—and by this time the hat
　　Was soiled and was bent, and renewal required:
So his successor washed it, and ironed it flat,
　　And with bows and with streamers he went forth attired.

Then the multitude hailed him a prodigy born,
　　His sires were as nothing, their deeds they were naught—
Thus it is with the dead—they are ever forlorn,
　　The present is all, while the past is forgot.

With philosophy, politics, all is the same,
　　Man lives in the littleness of his own day,
Unknown are the giants departed, to fame,
　　The living alone are the puppets that play.

　　　　　　　　　　　　　　　　GELLERT.

The Song of the Suabian Knight to his Son.

———∞∞∞———

Take my steed and lance, my son,
My course is o'er, my devoir done,
All too weighty now for me,
The warrior's arms and panoply.

Fifty years, these locks of grey
Have worn this helmet in the fray,
Every year the battle's brunt
Has left this axe and faulchion blunt.

'Twas Prince Rudolph, Suabia's Lord,
Girt me with this trusty sword,
'Twas to him my faith I vowed,
For Imperial gold too proud.

For the freedom of his land,
Rudolph gave his strong right hand,
With his left he broke the rank
Of the proud invading Frank.

Take these arms, my son, and wear,
The Emperor doth for war prepare,
Free me from these weapons weight,
For my age and strength too great.

Arm not in an evil cause,
Guard thy country's land and laws,
Be in council wise and cold,
In the strife as lion bold.

Ever hail the battle day,
Charge, where hottest is the fray,
Blench not from the arméd foe,
To the conquered mercy show.

When thy leagured banner droops,
Be a tow'r to guard thy troops,
Cheer them, dress them, and oppose
Serried ranks, to furious foes.

My son, seven youths, their country's pride,
Have fallen, fighting, by my side,
Thy mother sorrowing unto death,
Gave to grief her parting breath.

I am widowed and alone,
But my son, to thee, I own,
Thy disgrace would grieve me more,
Than thy brothers loss before.

Therefore, son, stern death defy,
Trust in God to live or die,
So thou bear thee as true knight,
Thou wilt be thy sire's delight.

FR: GRAF ZU STOLBERG. (A.D. 1138).

The Two Grenadiers.

Prisoners of war, two Grenadiers,
　　Towards France, from Russia toil,
With eyes cast down, and full of tears,
　　They tread the German soil.

For there they hear the tale of woe,
　　The tale of many a fray,
Their armies lost, and France laid low,
　　Their Emperor far away.

These Grenadiers they wept right sore,
　　While toiling on with pain,
Quoth one, "My tale of life is o'er,
　　" My wounds break out again."—

His comrade answered, " Woe is me !
　　" My race alike is run ;
" But, ah ! my wife and children three,
　　" Without me were undone."—

" Oh! what care I for child or wife,

"Woe, woe is me this day,

" My Emperor conquered in the strife,

" A captive far away!

"Grant me, my comrade, when I die,

" My bones in France to rest,

" Lay my good sword upon my thigh,

" My cross upon my breast.

" So will I watch within the tomb,

" Like sentry on his beat,

" Till I shall hear the cannon's boom,

" The war steed's trampling feet.

" Then o'er my grave with pomp of war,

" My Emperor shall ride,

" And I shall rise in arms once more,

" To battle by his side!"

HEINE.

The Black Knight.

'Twas Easter-tide in Hofburg's royal halls,
And joyous feasting reigned within its walls,
Then rose the good old King, and smiling said
"Bright dawn the Spring with blessings on each head!"

Now to the lists the trumpets summon loud,
And banners wave, crests glitter o'er the crowd,
With pride the Monarch from his throne looks down,
His son has all antagonists o'erthrown.

But see! a Knight advances to the fray
Dark as the grave. "Thy name and lineage say,"—
"Nay, at my name, ye all would look aghast,
"Suffice it, I am Prince of Kingdoms vast."

And as he paced the lists, the heavens grew black,
The castle shook, its walls were heard to crack ;
At the first charge the royal youth lay low,
And scarce could raise him from the unearthly blow.

U

Now fife and viol to the dance invite,
The royal halls with torch and brand are bright,
The boards with princely step the Black Knight treads,
And to the opening ball the Princess leads.

In helm of steel and armour darkly clad,
He threads the maze with solemn air and sad,
Cold is the arm, as ice, that wraps her form,
The flowers she wears drop withered as in storm.

Now to the board, with costly viands spread,
The lovely dames by noble knights are lead,
The good old King has eyes to mark alone
The much loved heir and heiress of his throne.

Pale and opprest the children both appear,
The King regards them with an anxious fear,
As the Black Knight presents with courtly air,
The golden cup to Prince and Princess fair.

And now upon their father's breast they lie,
The youth and maid in mortal agony,
The Sire hangs fondly on their parting breath,
And scarce resigns them to the arms of death.

"Wretch! thou hast lured thy victims to their doom,
"Now, bear their sorrowing parent to the tomb!"
"Man," said the arch fiend, "know'st thou not, in Spring
"I claim sweet roses for an offering."

UHLAND.

Little Roland.

In a cave in the rock Lady Bertha sate
Disconsolate, wailing her bitter fate,—
Young Roland her only son the while
Sported in childhood's innocent guile.—

"King Charles, my brother, noble and good,
"Why did I leave thy dear abode,
"For love I relinquished my rank and thee,
"And now my love has abandoned me.

"Oh! Milon, my husband fond and dear
"Cold art thou laid on thy watery bier,
"He for whose love I all resigned
"Has left me desolate here behind.

"Oh! Roland, Roland, my darling boy,
My bosom's treasure, my pride and joy,
"Come hither, come hither, quick to me,
"Thy mother has solace none but thee.

" My Roland, my Roland, go beg in the city,
" For wine and for food of their grace and pity,
" And forget not, in God's name, my darling to bless,
" The hand that shall minister to our distress."

King Charles he sat at his royal board,
Surrounded by many a knight and lord,
And around attendants many a score
The sparkling wines and rich viands bore,

Lutes and harps and minstrel's song
Gladdened the hearts of the joyous throng,
But never might note of mirth intrude
On Lady Bertha's solitude.

Many a beggar feasted there
Without the hall, on the goodly fare,
The bowl and platter to him were more
Than all the charms of the minstrel lore.

The King from his royal throne on high,
Surveys the scene with a curious eye,
And sudden sees thro' the serried mass
Threading his way, a stripling pass—

Of lovely face, and of bearing proud,
He tarries not with the humbler crowd,
But arrayed in garb of various hue,
To the royal board he pushes through.

Boldly he enters the princely hall,
Freely as tho' he were Lord of all,
He snatches a dish from the royal board
And bears it away without a word.

The King looks on with wondering eyes,
Amusement blending with surprize,
The rest observant of his mien
Smile blandly on the humorous scene

And soon again thro the open door,
The King beholds the boy once more,
He steps on the dais, and boldly takes up
The wondering Monarch's golden cup.

" How now, how now, thou impudent sprite !"
The King exclaims at the curious sight, —
The boy with innocent gaze looks up,
Still holding fast the golden cup.

The King at first looked stern and grave,
But soon a smile the child forgave,
" My child, these knightly halls you tread,
" As free as peasant walks the mead.

" You snatch the dishes from royalty,
" Freely as apples from the tree,
" You seize a flagon of muscatel,
" Freely as water from the well."—

" The serf from the well to fetch water is free,
" And gather ripe apples from the tree,
" But my sweet mother is worthy to share
" Your sparkling wines and your goodly fare."—

" And is thy mother a noble dame,
" As thy mien presumes, and thy words proclaim?
" And has she a castle and wide domain,
" And a noble court and princely train?

" Who is her steward? her cupbearer, who?
" Tell me, fair stripling, tell me true."—
" My right hand steward is to her,—
" My left hand is her cupbearer."—

" Who is her trusty sentinel?"—
" These blue eyes guard her true and well."—
" Who is her minstrel boy, declare?"—
" These lips for her make music rare."—

" Truly bold servants has the dame,
" And liveries strange her rank proclaim,
" Bright as the rainbow to behold,
" With colours rich and manifold."—

" Eight striplings from the neighbouring town
" I challenged, conquered, and struck down,
" And they as tribute, brought me store
" Of cloth to wear, of colours four."—

"Nay, to my mind, the lady boasts,
" The servant best in all my coasts,—
" Queen of the beggars, faith is she,
" And open house keeps royally ;

" A dame so noble is a star,
" That should not from my court be far ;
" Now, go my lords and ladies three,
" Conduct the dame in state to me."

Young Ronald, the golden cup he bears,
From the dais down the carpeted stairs,
Three noble lords, three ladies fair,
At the King's command they follow him there.

Small shadow the dial has cast—once more.
The King looks out through the open door,
And there returning in haste he spies
A goodly procession, with wondering eyes.

The lady she enters—the fairest of dames,—
" Now heaven forgive me," the King exclaims.
" In open hall without shame or grace
" I have mocked my own ancestral race.

" My sister, my sister, in pilgrim weed,
" With beggar's staff, can it be indeed
" In these princely halls ? now heaven forgive
" Such sight that I should see, and live."

Pale at his feet, Lady Bertha falls,
A piteous sight in those gilded halls,
The King—the cloud of his wrath is past,
On his sister's form he looks aghast.

Her eyes are closed and she dares not speak,
None may the solemn silence break,
Till the lovely boy, with his deep blue eyes,
Greets his fair uncle with joyous cries.

" Now raise thee, raise thee, sister mine,
" Thou fairest branch of our royal line,
" And for this sweet cherub's innocency
" All the past shall forgotten be."

With joy fair Bertha springs to her feet,
" Now brother bless thy words so sweet,
" My Roland shall pay thee loyally,
" For all the good thou hast done to me.

" His training shall be of the hero type,
" Till he grows like his King to a hero ripe,
" He shall conquer broad realms, and their banners bear
" On his blazoned shield, and his scutcheon fair.

" He shall rifle many a royal board,
" And humble the crest of knight and lord,
" And with spirit bold and strong right hand,
" Uphold and succour his Motherland."

UHLAND.

The Bell Founder of Breslau.

There dwelt of yore in Breslau's town
    A skilled artificer,
Enjoying all the high renown
    That art and craft confer.

Many a bell his hands had wrought,
    For church and chapel too,
Of metal bright, of every sort
    That rings most clear and true.

And ever pealed his bells so fair,
    So mellow, rich and bold,
It seemed that faith and love were there
    Commingled in the mould.

But of his bells the most far-famed,
    The bell that wore the crown,
It was "the Sinner's Bell," so named
    In Breslau's ancient town.

It hung in Magdalena's tow'r
    This master-piece of art,
Its deep and solemn sounds had pow'r
    To melt the hardest heart.

The master gave his thoughts by night,
    His hands for many a day,
To choose and mix the metal bright,
    And mould the form in clay.

And when it came the hour of birth,
    The metal mixed aright,
The mould embedded safe in earth,
    The furnace clear and bright ;

He called his young apprentice there,
    And bade him tend the fire,
Nor spare his watchful eye and care,
    Nor in his duty tire.

" For I am weary, faint and weak,
    " And need restoring power,
" Wine and refreshment I must seek
    " To nerve me for the hour.

" Yet, boy, beware you handle not
    " The spigot ere the time,
" Or yours will be a fearful lot,
    " For death will pay your crime."

The boy he stands intent beside
 The seething, melting mass,
He marks the whirling, eddying tide,
 That struggling boils to pass.

He hears it hiss, the metal pent,
 He groans in agony,
His fingers itch to ope the vent,
 And set the torrent free.

He feels the spigot in his hand—
 He turns it—and it flows—
His mind and reason lose command—
 He knows not what he does.—

He rushes forth to seek his chief,
 And tell the fearful news—
He clasps his knees in frantic grief,
 And loud for mercy sues.

But soon as e'er the Master heard
 His young apprentice tale,
His wrath o'ercame him at the word,
 His cheek grew deadly pale.

In maddening rage his blade he drew,
 And plunged it in his heart,
Then fled the fatal scene, to view
 The ruin of his art.

" Haply it may not be too late
   " The metal's flow to guide ; "
He looks! the stream has past the gate
   Into the mould beside.

He breaks the form—he clears the sand,
   He scarce can trust his sight ;
He sees the bell before him stand,
   Flawless and speckless bright.

The boy lies prostrate as in sleep,
   Unconscious on the ground,
" Oh ! Master, Master, all too deep,
   " Too fatal is the wound."—

The Master to the Judge proceeds,
   And tells his fearful tale—
For the good man, his kind heart bleeds,
   He listens sad and pale.

For naught can help him, nothing save,
   Blood must for blood atone—
He hears his sentence, calm and brave,
   As tho' his heart were stone.—

And when upon the fatal day,
   They led him forth to death,
And asked him, " Had he aught to pray ? "
   Ere he resigned his breath—

" My friends," he said, " most kind and true,
　　" I thank you for your grace ;
" For one small favour I would sue,
　　" If there be time and place.

" My latest work—that fatal bell,
　　" Its voice I yearn to hear
" Ring out my spirit's parting knell,
　　" In solemn tones and clear."—

Freely 'twas granted, boon so small,
　　And as he went to death,
The solemn dirge was heard by all,
　　'Twas heard with bated breath.

The Master, too, he heard the peal
　　Sound forth so rich and clear,
He seemed an inward joy to feel,
　　Despite the falling tear.

And in his eyes there dawned a light,
　　By inspiration fired,
It was for mortal joy too bright,
　　It seemed of heaven inspired.

Then on the block his head he laid,
　　With courage calm and bold,—
With death was his transgression paid,
　　His name in heaven enrolled.

That, of his bells, which to this hour.
Enjoys the most renown,
It hangs in Magdalena's tower,
In Breslau's ancient town.

From that day forth, for long I know.
'Twas called "The Sinner's Bell,"
But an it bears that title now,
Gentles, I cannot tell.

MÜLLER.

Retribution.

Through the dark mazes of the wood,
    The Squire paced slow the Knight beside,
With envious eyes, in evil mood,
    Thirsting, a knight himself, to ride.

With dastard hand his blade he drew,
    And plunged it in the good Knight's side,
Then stripped his plated mail and threw,
    The lifeless corpse in Rhine's swift tide.

Then in the good Knight's arms arrayed,
    He mounted light his noble steed,
And threaded swift the forest glade,
    And gaily crossed the grassy mead.

But as his footsteps clattered o'er
    The bridge on Rhine's blue stream so slight,
Ere he had gained the farther shore,
    The charger swerved and reared upright.

He spurred the steed, he reared again,
    The rider from his seat was thrown,
He struggled with the waves in vain,
    The pond'rous armour weighed him down.

UHLAND.

The Mother and Child.

Mother.

My child, the angels took thy brother,
Because he never grieved thy mother.

Child.

Oh ! tell me, mother, how to grieve thee
That I may never, never leave thee.

UHLAND.

The Lurlei.

My heart is sad, I know not why —
The passing Zephyr seems a sigh !
The shadow of a tale of woe
Rests on my mind from long ago.—

    'Tis twilight—on the banks of Rhine
    The stars like glittering diamonds shine—
    The sun-set on the mountains glows,
    While at their feet the current flows.—

    Above—a maiden wondrous fair
    Sits combing soft her golden hair,
    Chaunting with melody divine,
    While her rich robes with jewels shine.—

    The sailor—in his bark below,
    Heeds not the waters as they flow—
    His gaze is on the maid so fair—
    Her locks, her song, have witched him there.—

    He sees nor wave, nor sunken rock,
    He hears no sound, he feels no shock,
    Lured by the Lurlei's fatal charms,
    He sleeps his death sleep in her arms !

HEINE.

The Traveller.

A traveller sped on his weary way,
Ths sun forgot to shine that day,
The traveller drenched with chilling rain,
To Jupiter loudly did complain—
Jove answered not—the rain did pour,
With lightning flash and thunder's roar,
And ever to Jove, as the weather grew worse,
The traveller uttered a bitterer curse.
At length in a shady wood hard by
He thought to cheat the watery sky,
But there, a brigand in ambush lay,
To watch the road, and seize his prey—
He fixed his arrow, and drew his bow,
But the string was wet, with the rain and snow,
And despite the robber's skill and craft
He missed his aim with the erring shaft.—
Oh! fool, said Jove, art thou now content,?
Had the sun but shone, when that bow was bent,
That arrow had pierced thy heart this day,
And thou had'st fallen the brigand's prey!

GELLERT.

The Faithful Monkey.

———◦✦◦———

Four bearers bore a palanquin,
　　From Delhi to Lahore,
A Hindoo merchant sat therein,
　　Behind, four bearers more.

Upon the roof a monkey sat,
　　As jaunty as you please,
In scarlet mantle and cocked hat,
　　A gentleman at ease.

Six robbers from the jungle rushed—
　　Down dropped the palanquin—
The bearers and the monkey brushed—
　　The first, no more were seen.

The robbers dragged the old man out,
　　And killed him then and there,
Then tore from off his person stout
　　His gold and jewels rare.

They dug a hole and laid him in,
    The plunder too they buried,
Then disappeared, the jungle in,
    And thro' its mazes scurried.

The monkey sitting in a tree,
    Beheld the whole affair,
And when the robbers bolted, he
    Began to curse and swear

In monkey-tongue, of course I mean,
    Darwin would understand it,
Certes, he vented all his spleen,
    Upon the murderous bandit.

Then with a solemn look and sly,
    Pug skipped along the road,
To where a station stood hard by,
    And the police abode.

There such a chatter he began,
    As made them think him crazed,
He howled, grimaced and skipped and ran,
    Till all were fairly mazed.

But soon he made them understand
    They were to follow him,
And forth he led the wondering band,
    Into the jungle dim.

And there he stopped beside a grave,
    And scratched and howled like mad,
The lookers on who heard him rave,
    It made them all quite sad.

But soon they got a spade and dug,
    And found the poor old man,
And when he saw him, faithful Pug
    To howl afresh began.

Poor Pug! they bore him struggling home—
    He neither slept nor fed—
But forth, by day and night, would roam
    Heedless of board and bed.

'Twas sad to see him pine away,
    Listless and wan and thin—
'Twas sad to see him day by day,
    In hopeless misery grin.

At last, one morn, his guardian kind
    Went to a neighbouring town,
He would not leave poor Pug behind,
    He was so helpless grown.

Pug in his arms—around he stares,
    Pacing the gay bazaar,
Admiring all the costly wares,
    And treasures from afar.

Sudden the monkey with a cry,
    Springs to the ground beneath,
And fixes on a passer by,
    And holds him with his teeth !

In vain he screamed, in vain he swore,
    Pug dauntless kept his hold,
Till man and monkey on the floor,
    In mad confusion rolled.

They tore him off by force at length,
    And tried his wrath t'assuage,
But still he struggled might and strength,
    With unabated rage.

The crowd, as crowds will do, began
    To question, reason, pry,
The monkey first, and then the man,
    Each was a mystery.

Pug's guardian told the murderous tale,
    And how the monkey pined,
'Twas clear, the man who grew so pale
    Had something on his mind.

So then they charged him home, and bade
    His murderous deed confess—
While he, bewildered and dismayed,
    Stood in mute wretchedness.

Then next they bade his comrades tell,
　　And seized, and bound them all,
And dragged them where the old man fell,
　　And there—they hanged them all !

Poor Pug looked on with solemn mien,
　　His master's grave beside,
Then turned him from the sickening scene,
　　And moaned, and gasped,—and died.

The German Rhine.

The Rhine!—the Rhine!—
The German Rhine!—
They shall not have the German Rhine.—
Tho' like the ravens, they croak themselves hoarse for it—
Long as the plashing echoes of oars in it,
Long as it glides, thro' its gardens of vine—
Ne'er shall they have it—the free German Rhine!

The Rhine! the Rhine!
The glorious Rhine!—
They shall not have the German Rhine—
Long as its golden waves gladden the heart,
Till its gaunt rocks from their firm bases start,
Long as it mirrors castle and shrine—
Ne'er shall they have it—the free German Rhine!

The Rhine! the Rhine!
The glorious Rhine!—
They shall not have the German Rhine—
Long as bold youths woo maidens more fair,
Long as its fishes leap high in the air,
Long as its minstrels sing music divine—
Till it coffins the bones of the last of our line—
They never shall have it—the free German Rhine!

NICHOLAS BECKER.

The Song of the Bell.

—⚬⚬⦂⊶⦂⚬⚬—

Deep embedded in the earth
    The clay burnt mould is set,
To-day the Bell must have its birth—
    Comrades to the work well met !

From your foreheads, perspiration
    Must in streams unstinted flow :
Earn the master's approbation—
    The blessing comes not from below !

Earnest words, and good discourse
    Beseem the work we have on hand ;
Labour best pursues its course,
    When sage converse cheers the band.

So, gravely friends, consider now
    The ills that from weak counsels flow ,
Worthless the man that ponders not
    The cares and duties of his lot !

The powers of man's intelligence,
　　His reason, and his soul, were given,
That he might yield his mind and sense
　　To the pursuits imposed by Heav'n.

　　Take the logs of pinewood dry,
　　Pile them up, and pile them high,
　　That the flame confined
　　May the opening find—
　　To the molten mass,
　　　　Cast the ingots in
　　　　That the copper and the tin,
　　May in due proportion pass.—

The bell, that with the help of fire
　　We fashion in the mould,
Shall in the belfry's height aspire
　　To counsel young and old.

To many an age 'twill tell its tale,
　　'Twill strike the ears of many a mortal,
'Twill sadly with the afflicted wail,
　　And to devotion ope the portal.

The changing scenes of life below,
　　Its incidents of joy or woe,
The sounding metal loud shall ring
　　And far and wide the message wing.

See white flames are rising high,
　　Showing that the mixture flows!
Haste, wood ashes to supply,
　　So, the liquid smoother goes.
Free from scum the stream should be,
That the clangor full and free,
May ring out melodiously.

Now with welcome loud and deep,
　　The new-born babe it ushers in,
Entering in the arms of sleep
　　On this world of pain and sin.
For it, as yet, life's joys and woes
In the womb of time repose—
A mother's love, of heaven born,
Watches o'er life's early morn—
The seasons, swift as arrow, glide,
The youth soon quits the young girl's side,
And on life's journey thro' the land,
Forth he goes with staff in hand—
A stranger, to his home returns,
　　And in joyous manhood's pride,
He seeks with cheek that blushing burns
　　The blooming maiden at his side.
A nameless longing fills his heart,
　　And tears bedew his eyes,

He wanders forth—alone—apart
    And from his comrades flies.

He tracks her steps, where'er she goes,
    Enraptured when they meet,
And culls the loveliest flower that blows,
    To cast it at her feet.

Oh fond delight—delicious hope—
    Of first love's golden day,
The eye beholds the heavens ope,
    The heart seems steeped in bliss for aye.

The tubes are browning—see I thrust
This little rod beneath the crust—
When we see it glisten,
Listen, comrades, listen!
The casting time is come—
Prove the metal, watch the scum—
See if hard, with soft, combines
For the work, with goodly signs.

When weak and strong united meet,
    Harmonious is the song,
Let those who bind themselves for aye,
    With prudent care essay,
If heart to heart, responsive beat—
    Fancy is brief, repentance long!

In the bridal tresses bright,
    Shines the marriage garland's sheen,
When the merry peals invite,
    To the gay and festive scene.
Alas! with virgin love's May-day,
Fades life's brightest dream away.
With the veil and with the zone,
Is the lovely vision flown
    Passion must pass away,
    Love must for ever stay—
The flower must die, the fruit must grow—
Forth into life the man must go—
    He must work, and must strive,
    Must plan, and contrive,
    He must risk, and must snatch,
    Good fortune to catch—
    Thus only, possessions grow,
    Granaries overflow,
    Houses more spacious show—
    In them, the housewife rules,
    As mother, the children schools—
    So wise is her reign
    In the household domain !
        The maidens she teaches,
        To the young lads, she preaches,
    And ceaseless she drives
    The men and the wives,

She increases the gains
With her orderly pains,
The stores without measure
She heaps up with treasure,
The spindle she plies,
Whirring swift as it flies,
Of linen of snow, and glittering wool,
That the presses and chests, of the best, shall be full.
She is careful and clever,
And rests herself—never!
And the good man in pride
From his gable, below,
Looks out far and wide,
Where the trelissed vines grow,
And the barns overflowing
Rich blessings bestowing.

Like waves on the ocean
His corn, zephyrs kiss,
And his heart, with emotion,
Boasts loud of his bliss.
So full is his cup
That his house seems set up
As firm as a rock,
'Gainst adversity's shock—
But alas! with prosperity
None can make bond,

Swift cometh adversity,
Looming beyond!

The casting, now, may be begun,
The metal mixes fair,
Yet before we let it run—
Pray we an earnest prayer—

Draw the spigot out!
God the household save!
Smoking from the spout
Shoots the fiery wave!

Fire is a blessing true,
Controlled and used aright,
For mortals' grandest works are due
To its heaven-gifted might—

Yet fearful, when in luckless hour
It bursts its shackles, is that power,
And rushes on its headlong course,
Nature's child in native force!
And woe, when unrestrained and free
The flames rush on increasingly,
Mad, without remorse or pity,
Careering through the crowded city,
When the elements conspire,
With the wild devouring fire.

From the clouds,
Whose veil enshrouds,
   Blessing comes at last!
The rain down pours,
The tempest roars,
   The bolts from heaven are cast
Hark how the storm mutters,
   High from the tower—
      Blood red the heaven—
The bright light that flutters—
   Is not day's power—
      The earth and the heaven
      With turmoil are riven—
The vapour upcurls,
The lurid flame whirls—
Thro' the long winding street,
The wind fans the heat—
   Like oven's mouth racking,
   Rafters crashing, windows cracking,
   Children screaming, mothers crying
   Beasts beneath the ruins lying,
   Groaning, struggling desperately,
   Burst their bonds and set them free
      The darksome night
      Is mid-day bright—
   From hand, to hand, the buckets fly,
   And jets of water mount on high,

Howling comes the stormy wind—
The bristling flame speeds fast behind
Crackling in the garners dry,
It seeks the faggots piled on high,
And as tho' in its mad flight
T'would bear away earth's stored up might,
It swells to giant height.—
    Man beneath God's judgment quails,
    And the dire disaster wails !

Charred and gutted is the pile,
    Destroying angels fitting bed,
In the vacant casement, while
    Horror rears her ghastly head,
And within the empty space
Sky and air alone have place.

On the grave of his belongings
    One last look the good man sends,
Then despite his spirit's longings
    Staff in hand, his way he wends—
'Mid the direful conflagration
Still remains one consolation,
    Of the loved ones in his hall
None is wanting to his call !

The stream is forth, the mould is full,
    So far is the task propitious,

A A

Pray the metal softly cool,
  And our skill and toil enrich us-
  Should the torrent stray,
  Should the mould give way !—
Alas ! how oft when hope beguiles,
Disaster lurks beneath her smiles !

In earth's prolific womb we lay
  Our hopes of growing store,
The sower strews his seed in clay,
  Trusting in heaven to gather more—
Weeping, a costlier seed we lay
In earth's dark lap of kindred clay,
And hope from out the dreary tomb
Immortal flowers shall rise and bloom !

From the steeple, hark the bell,
Deep and earnest, sounds the knell—
  That solemn toll
  A parting soul
Ushers on the untrodden road
Leading to its last abode !

Forth the deadly arrow flew—
Spouse beloved, and mother true—
Ah ! the shaft was aimed—at you !
  See the King of Terrors tear

The victim from the husband's arms,
From the loved ones whom she bare,
Memorials of her early charms
Whom she watched with mother's zest.
Growing on her anxious breast—
Since, alas, the watchful mother
Guards no more the sacred hearth,
That, supplanted by another,
She must tread a Spirit's path,
The household bond is rent for ever,
To be re-united—never !

Rest we while the bell is cooling
Like the birds disporting free,
Joyous all in bush and tree.
As at vesper, from their schooling
Boys by starlight shout with glee,
While the master, never free,
Ever watches anxiously !

In the forest's darkling glade
Deepens fast the evening shade,
As the wand'rer wends his way
To his home at close of day—
Bleating flocks and lowing kine,
Tread the roads in lengthened line,
To the accustomed fold and stall
Sheep, and oxen, hasten all.

Waggons groan beneath the weight
Of the harvest's golden freight—
On the topmost sheaf of all
Rests the flow'ry coronal,
And the reapers to the dance,
Youth and maid, in bands advance—
Street and market, now are still,
    The city gates with pondrous jar,
Close, while lighted chambers fill
    With citizens and guests from far—
Earth herself in sable decks,
Naught of night the burgher recks,
For him the eye of justice wakes,
The bad alone, in darkness quakes.

Holy order, blessing rife!
Heaven's fair daughter, foe to strife!
Which can men, with fetters light,
In harmonious bond unite—
Only safe, and sure, foundation
For the building of a nation,
Which, the savage erst beguiled
From his desert and his wild,
And in human dwelling placed
    Which, for him, with gentle hand,
Fondly wove, and interlaced,
    The sacred bond of fatherland.

One common yoke of union binds
Thousands of active hands and minds—
The master, and the servant, too,
Alike, the ends of life pursue,
    'Neath freedom's sacred banner,
Each to their several interests true,
    Each in their several manner.
The subject's craft is his renown,
    His toil-devoted hours—
The monarch's honour is his crown,
    Our handiwork is ours—

Oh! holy concord—blessed Peace!
To guard our city never cease,
Nor ever dawn the dreadful hour
When war its savage hordes shall pour
Adown this peaceful vale, which now,
Blushes with the sunset glow,
And the lurid sky shall lower
With smoke and flame from wall and tower!

Now break the mould—its task is done—
    Now feast our hearts and eyes,
Upon the work, whose course is run,
    With joy and glad surprise—
        Swing the hammer, swing!
        Till the metal ring,

Till its grasp the clay releases,
 Ere it sees the light—the bell
 Must break its brittle shell,
And its covering fall to pieces.

At fitting time, the master may
Fearless, destroy the crust of clay,
 But woe, when the glowing ore
 Finds for itself a door,
 And rushes forth with thunder's roar
As from hell's wide jaws outpouring
Tongues of flame to heaven upsoaring —
When force, unbridled, holds command
No edifice can hope to stand,
And when, against the powers that be,
The masses rise tumultuously,
No Commonwealth can prosperous be —
Woe, when disaffection reigns,
 In the bosom of the State,
 When the people burst their chains,
 And in deadly wrath and hate,
  In luckless hour—
  Seize the power—
And sound the note of war
With harsh and hideous jar
Upon the mellow bell, but late
To peace and concord dedicate—

" Freedom and equality "—
Howling comes the cry—
The burghers rush to arms,
The street with people swarms—
The slums let loose their horde
And murder stalks abroad.
Women, like hyænas laughing,
Grim, at scenes of direst woe,
Panther-like, the heart's blood quaffing
Of the dead and mangled foe—
Naught is sacred, hence for ever,
The bonds of sanctity must sever.
Good gives place to evil—vice
Reigns, like hell, in paradise.—
Fearful is the tiger's spring,
    The lion's open portal,
But of all the deadliest thing
    Is the rage of angry mortal!—
Alas! the lovers of their kind,
Who prematurely haste to find
Light and instruction for the blind,
But dazzle only, and o'erwhelm,
In fire and ashes town and realm!—

    Heaven the work has sped—
      Like a golden star
      Shining from afar,

The husk, the nut has shed—
From crown to rim it gleams
Like the sun's bright beams.
While the arms on the blazoned shield,
Just honor to the master yield !
Hither, hither, come to call,
Close the circle, comrades all !
While we consecrate the Bell—
Let its name " Concordia " be,
So, to the neighbours shall it tell
Its tale of peace and harmony !

And this shall be its proud vocation,
The master's fondest aspiration,
High above this nether sphere,
In heaven's blue vault, so still and clear,
With voice as solemn, deep and loud
As issues from the thunder-cloud,
The great Creator's praise to sound :
And as the year rolls swiftly round,
Echo the music of the stars,
Revolving on their glittering cars—
Its brazen voice we dedicate,
To register decrees of fate,
And hourly with its tuneful chime
To mark the rapid flight of time—

Itself, unknowing sympathy,
Shall speak the voice of destiny,
Shall note the course of human life,
Of change and trouble ever rife,
And as its deep tones on the ear,
Vibrate with feelings kin to fear,
Let each his lesson learn—on earth
That all is transient—grief and mirth,
And death as certain as our birth !

Now the ropes with vigour ply,
See, it moves—it mounts on high,
To the realms of sound !
Heaven on us its blessings send,
Happiness our State attend,
Joy and peace abound !

SCHILLER.

The Sad Tournament.

Seven knights rode forth, so bold and free,
In arms accoutred, cap à pie,
    A knightly tournament to hold,
In honour of their Lady love,
For whom they pined, for whom they strove,
    The daughter of a monarch old.

Castle and rampart soon they gained,
And when their noble steeds they reined,
    They heard the tinkling of a bell,
And as they trod the royal hall,
On marble floor and sable pall,
    The light of seven torches fell.

And there they saw laid out in state
As monument inanimate
    The fair and lovely Adelaide—
While at her head, in speechless woe,
Her royal sire sat bending low,
    Wailing the sweet departed maid.

Then out spoke Degenworth the bold,
" No fairer form this earth did hold :
 " How lovely still in death's cold sleep !
 " Alas that we have armed in vain,
" And mounted steed and slackened rein,
 " For I must ever mourn and weep."

Then spoke the young Lord Adelbert—
" Nor death, nor sorrow, should divert
 " Our fondly purposed enterprize—
" Worthy is yonder maid indeed,
" That we for her should fight and bleed,
 " Though lost for ever to our eyes."

Then spoke Sir Walther, noble knight—
" Now vain it were for us to fight
 " For one who reigns a saint above,
" Better to yield the bootless quest
" And homeward bending seek for rest,
 " In mem'ry of our lady love."

Then answered Adelbert the bold—
" 'Tis true the maid lies dead and cold,
 " But never maiden was so fair,
" Against you all the lists I'll hold,
" If only for her ring of gold,
 " And for the roses in her hair."

Then forth they rode upon the sand,
And straight encountered hand to hand,
    Defying wounds and cruel fate.
And soon six champions of the seven
Found death on earth and rest in heaven,
    While one in selle sore wounded sate.

The seventh was Lord Adelbert,
Bravest of all and most expert—
    Down slipped he, from his charger pale—
And as he crossed the royal hall,
And by the torchlight viewed the pall,
    His trembling footsteps seemed to fail.

He snatched the wreath of roses red,
And golden circlet from the dead,
    Then sunk to earth, like blighted bloom—
The King in robe of sable clad,
To raise the six dead champions bad,
    And followed mourning to their tomb.

Six knights were they of courage rare,
The seventh Count Adelbert lay there,
    Beside his own sweet Adelaide—
They placed them in a single grave,
The lovely maid—the youth so brave—
    And on their tomb one stone they laid.

                    UHLAND.

The Richest Prince.

———◦◦◦———

In Worms' imperial hall of state,
At banquet high, the princes sate,
And each aglow with cup in hand,
Vaunted the merits of his land.

First spoke the Prince of Saxony—
" Riches and power belong to me,
" For wealth untold of precious ore
" Deep in my mountains lies in store."

Then said the Elector of the Rhine—
" Mine is a land of corn and wine,
" The valleys wave with golden grain
" And purple grapes their summits stain."

Next Louis spoke, Bavaria's Lord—
" In towns and monasteries stored,
" My Kingdom boasts a wealth as great
" Of gold and art as any State."

Then gravely rose, with flowing beard,
Of Wirtemburg, Prince Eberherd—
" My realm with cities, riches, mines,
" Nor treasured art luxurious shines.

" Yet hoard have I of wealth more sure,
" Than corn or wine, or metal pure,
" In forest dark my head may rest,
" Pillowed on serf or noble's breast."

Then cried those Lords of kingdoms three,
Bavaria, Rhine, and Saxony,
" Prince of the beard, the laurels wear,
" Thy soil is rich in jewels rare."

JUSTINUS KERNER.

The Song of a Brave Man.

———∞∞⚬❧❀⚬∞∞———

The worthiest theme for lute or lyre,
For poet's lay, or minstrel's fire,
   Is praise of noble deed,
By men who toil in honour's cause,
Nor covet guerdon, or applause—
   Of such, is now my rede.

The melting breath of spring's first breeze,
Came sweeping o'er the southern seas,
   Thro' Italy's fair plain ;
The fleecy clouds before it fled,   ·
Like flocks by hungry wolves bestead,
   And ice gave place to rain.

The hills had doffed their veil of snow.
A thousand torrents coursed below,
   Adown the mountain's side.
A mighty lake the stream replaced,
That with its bordering meadows graced
   The valley's verdant pride.

With buttress strong, and arch of stone,
Across the stream a bridge was thrown,
    And in its centre stood
A hut, where dwelt a frail old man,
With wife, and child of scarce a span,
    The Guardian of the road.

The tempest roars, the arches quake,
The billows heave, the rafters shake,
    Upon the roof he stands,
He gazes round with aspect wild,
"Oh, save them, save my wife and child!"
He cries with outstretched hands.

The solid wall on either side
Goes down before the surging tide,
    And now the arches fall;
But mid the crash of broken beams
And howling blast, the wretches' screams
    Are heard above them all.

Borne by the torrent, pile on pile,
The ice in masses huge the while
    Rends buildings, plank and beam;
Till swept by wave, by boulders reft,
The central arch alone is left,
    An islet in the stream.

And now upon the further strand,
A gaping crowd is seen to stand,
　　And shout and ring their hands ;
Yet all in vain the prisoners shriek
For aid and help, that crowd so weak
　　Infirm of purpose stands.

But ah, see now, on charger proud,
A noble Baron, shouting loud
　　Above the tempest's roar,
" This purse to him, the bold, the brave,
" Who will those wretched inmates save
　　And bring them to the shore!"

Right noble Baron, free of hand
And heart—an honor to thy land,
　　I give thee worship due!
But loftier must my muse aspire,
To sing with concentrated fire,
　　A worthier man than you.

And ever higher swells the flood,
And fiercer still the tempest's mood,
　　And nearer death appears,
A moment lost—what hope to save
Those shrinking victims from the grave
　　And dry their falling tears !

C C

Again the Baron proffers loud
His golden guerdon to the crowd,
    They hear, but turn away.
And still the prisoners shrieks are heard,
Borne on the blast like wail of bird
    Amid the drifting spray.

But ah ! see there, from out the crowd,
Of lowly garb, but bearing proud,
    A peasant youth emerge ;
He heard the Count and understood,
He boldly gazed upon the flood,
    And scanned the boiling surge.

Then, in God's name, despite the blast,
His form, into a boat, he cast,
    And gained the tottering wall.
But all too frail the shallop seemed,
Too weak to breast the waves, he deemed
    He might not save them all.

And thrice, his boat he dauntless rows,
Tho' whirlpool boils and tempest blows,
    And thrice, has reached the land ;
Then leaning breathless on his oar,
He marks the building topple o'er,
    And crumble into sand.

Who is it, who? this brave man, say,
Proclaim it now, my faithful lay—
　　"A peasant true and bold."
The Baron proffered noble wage,
The peasant, frank, took up the guage—
　　Was it for love of gold?

The Baron spoke, "Now, worthy son,
"Take thy reward, 'twas bravely won,
　　"And with it goes my heart."
Right noble was that Baron's will,
The peasant's heart was nobler still.
　　His was a grander part.

"'Tis true," he said, "My lot is low,
"Nor wealth nor luxury I know;
　　"I risked not life for gold!
"Yield it to him, who all has lost,
"Whose household gods are tempest tost"—
　　He turned—my tale is told.

BÜRGER.

The Pilgrim of St. Just.

'Tis night, and the demon of storms is unchained,
    A traveller stands at the gate,
And now it is opened—the threshold is gained,—
    "What would ye, sir stranger, so late?"

"Sir Abbot I come as a brother to crave,
    "The lot of your order to share,
"Let me rest in a cell, dark and cold, as the grave,
    "Till the matin bell summons to pray'r.

"The garb of your order—a coffin—and cell
    "Are all that I ask of your grace,
"Tho' the world lay but yesterday under my spell,
    "And I governed the whole human race.

"This head, that for cowl, and for tonsure, is bowed,
    "An imperial diadem bore,
"This form, that a cassock of serge will enshroud,
    "Imperial ermine once wore.

"And now, I come hither, to waste, and to die,
    "To mingle my bones with the clay,
"In the tomb's cold obstruction to rot and to lie,
    As my kingdoms have crumbled away.

PLATEN.

The Artful Thief.

A cunning old thief to confessional went,
Absolution to seek for his past errors bent,
But, as ill-luck would have it, the Priest had a watch.
Which, the force of old habit, enjoined him to snatch.
So he knelt at the feet of the pious old man,
And thus his design and confession began :
" My father, I steal,"—and his light fingers stole
To the chain which was fixed in the neat button hole.—
" Nay, speak not, my son, of the present—but say,
" *I have stolen*—forgive me, my father. I pray."—
Meantime, the gold watch, the old thief made his own,—
" Yes father, I've stolen, my crime I bemoan."
" Well, tell me the tale—from concealment refrain "—
" Nay father, I've stolen a watch and a chain."—
" My son, the lost goods to their owner restore "—
" Nay, father, to thee will I now hand them o'er."
" My son, I decline them—thy conscience inspires
" To the owner to yield them, and duty requires."—
" My father, I've done so, but he doth decline."—
" Then retain them, my son, thou may'st keep them as thine.
He ended—the thief took his leave, and was gone,
'Twas twilight around him, the Priest was alone.
He felt for his watch with its golden-linked chain—
They are gone !—he shall welcome them never again !
Thus, when least we expect to encounter a cross,
The moment is big with disaster and loss.

BÜRGER

Corporal Spohn.

In fair Coblentz, the name is known,
Of great and famous Corporal Spohn—
Now, what was Spohn, that his memory lies
Embalmed in his country's admiring eyes?
Spohn was a man, as true and brave,
As ever *slept in* soldier's grave ;
He served and followed—faithful Spohn—
An Emperor named Napoleon,
Who, in the war of Emperors three,
Had pushed too far, too heedlessly,—
And thus it was, that watchful foes,
To right, and left, his way enclose—
A horde of Cossacks scoured the plain,
The Emperor saw, and fled amain ;
But bush and thicket barred the way,
And death confronted him that day.—
Spohn saw, and swift as lightning cried,
" Thy horse, thy hat, dismount and ride,
" With thy famed hat, thy well-known steed,
" I will the savage foe mislead."

Then sprang to earth Napoleon,
And on his steed mounts gallant Spohn.—
Upon the track the Cossacks speed,
They knew the hat, the milk-white steed.—
They close around him, seize their prey,
While fast the Emperor speeds away.
But when they find him all alone,
They hew him down, poor Corporal Spohn!
Swift to the lines the Emperor sped,
The Corporal's hat upon his head.—
And from that day, his name from all,
Was this—" the little Corporal,"—
The true, great Corporal was Spohn,
The *lesser* was Napoleon!

KARL SIMROCK

The Lord of Falkenstein.

Forth rides the Lord of Falkenstein,
Thro' meadows rich with corn and wine,
   A glad and glorious scene—
What vision fair confronts his sight?—
A maid, in robes, like lily white,
   And locks of golden sheen.

"Sweet maid, what dost thou here this day,
"Alone and unprotected, say—
   "Oh wouldst thou be my bride?—
"Then quickly mount my gallant steed,
"And pace with me the grassy mead
   "And to my castle ride."—

"Nay, bride of thine, I ne'er will be,
"Nor homeward will I ride with thee,
   "Sir knight I know thee not."—
"Yet I am Lord of Falkenstein,
"Descendant of a noble line,
   "A name, by few, forgot."

"Nay, art thou Lord of Falkenstein,
"And art thou of that noble line?
　"Then in thy dungeons lies
"A youth, thy prisoner, dear to me,
"Oh draw the bolts and set him free,
　"The jewel of my eyes."

"Maiden, my castle vaults are deep,
"Its walls are massive, high and steep,
　"There, let thy lover lie,"—
"Nay, if thy heart be hard as stone,
'I'll seek thy prisoner's dungeon lone,
　"And give him, sigh for sigh."

And there beneath those towers she strays,
And fondly weeps, and sighs and prays,
　"My loved one art thou here?
"This heart will break, this brain will turn,
"So much to see thy face I yearn,
　"To hear thy voice so dear.

"Oh had I weapons, lance and sword,
"I'd meet thee, false and cruel Lord,
　"And brave thee hand to hand "—
"Nay, maid, 'twere shame to fight with thee,
"But I will set thy lover free,
　"If thou wilt quit the land."

" What! leave my father's house, and home,
" And as a thief and exile roam,
 " Nay never while I live ?"
" Well maid, thy faith and constancy
" Have won the fight, and conquered me.—
 " Thy love to thee I give!"

KARL SIMROCK.

The Timid Lover.

I loved thee—oh, I loved thee well,
I longed to speak, but dared not tell,
    The secret of my heart,—
I sought a time, to shew my flame,
Alas! the time it never came,
    I felt the hour depart.

Another came—he tarried not—
Fortune befriends the venturous lot,—
    He won and wears the prize.
Love thee he may—I cannot tell—
Not more than I—if half as well,
    My wounded spirit sighs.

REINECKE.